AROUND
ORPINGTON
THROUGH TIME
Phil Waller

AMBERLEY PUBLISHING

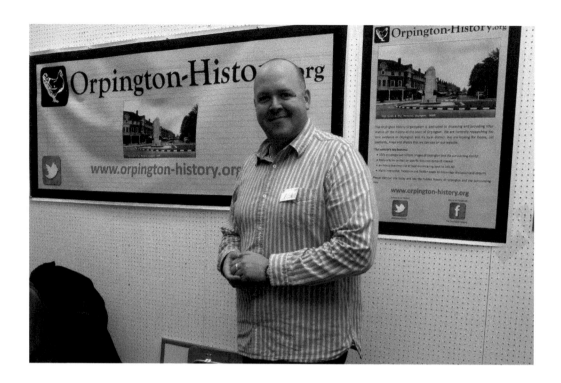

To Jen, without whose love and support this book would not have existed, and to Charlie, our son, the newest resident of Orpington.

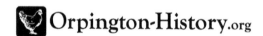 Orpington-History.org

First published 2013

Amberley Publishing
The Hill, Stroud, Gloucestershire, GL5 4EP
www.amberley-books.com

Copyright © Phil Waller, 2013

The right of Phil Waller to be identified as the
Author of this work has been asserted in accordance with
the Copyrights, Designs and Patents Act 1988.

ISBN 978 1 4456 1767 1 (print)
ISBN 978 1 4456 1785 5 (ebook)

British Library Cataloguing in Publication Data.
A catalogue record for this book is available from the
British Library.

Typesetting by Amberley Publishing.
Printed in Great Britain.

Introduction

Modern Orpington and its district, as we know it, has not yet reached its centenary. The history of Orpington, however, goes much further back. Generations of local historians have enjoyed and spent countless hours researching and recording information and pictures using the available methods of the day to show their work to anyone who might be interested. The sharing of their knowledge with others often took the form of local publications, talks in village halls and exhibitions at larger local events. The enthusiasm and need to research has not really changed, but the use of modern technology to find out more and the ability to share their findings more widely has. Philip Waller, author of *Around Orpington Through Time*, brought two of his hobbies together to establish the online Orpington History Organisation (OHO). A native of Orpington, he has a keen interest in local history going back nearly twenty-five years, combined with success in running large online internet-based communities and groups.

The Orpington History Organisation (www.orpington-history.org) began with a website page offering a detailed timeline, a collection of hundreds of pictorial items and a very successful social media channel. This initial beginning was embraced and expanded by the interaction of enthusiasts who became an integral part of the organisation in terms of contributions, both verbally and through pictorial submissions. The purpose of the OHO was to fill a missing gap on the internet with the objective to share a good portion of its collection, display articles and generate interaction. Since its creation in 2006, the OHO has gone from strength to strength with its extremely popular website, talks and exhibitions and huge international following on Facebook and Twitter. The Orpington History Organisation is also proud to be a founder member of the Bromley Heritage and Arts Forum.

All old images, apart from those credited throughout the book, are part of the Orpington History Organisation Collection. The modern images, unless credited otherwise, were taken by Tom Yeeles and Phil Waller – all rights are reserved.

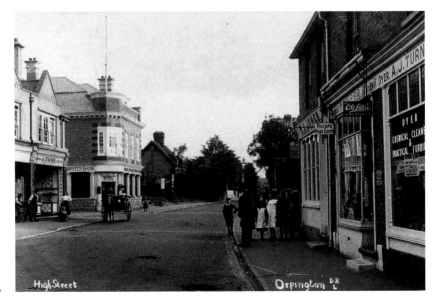

Orpington high Street, around 1915, at the junction of Homefield Rise.

Foreword

At first glance, Orpington may appear to the visitor to be quite an ordinary, typical suburban town. However, look a bit deeper and you will see that the development of Orpington and the surrounding district has a very interesting history. Prehistoric remains were found here and Iron Age remains and Dene holes appear all over the area. Land ways that have been used for possibly thousands of years continue to exist. Queen Elizabeth I visited here during her reign. An important feature is the old priory and gardens, which are over 700 years old. Charles Darwin, Sir John Lubbock, George Allen and Brass Crosby are among many famous people who made their homes in the district.

For many centuries, farms in the district produced some of the finest crops and livestock in the country. William Cook produced the internationally famous Orpington chicken. George's Famous Pork Sausages were produced at Tripes Farm and sold all over the Empire. The River Cray was dominated by large mills and factories. Fox & Sons Oak Brewery was based at Green Street Green. Allied Bakeries, one of the biggest commercial bakeries in the UK, has been here for nearly eighty years. The Cray Industrial Estate provided a huge number of jobs to skilled, local workers. Factories produced everything from records to weighing machines; electronics components to industrial dyes and paints. The First and Second World Wars had an impact on the district in different ways. A Canadian Military Hospital dominated the area for some considerable time and evolved into the current Orpington Hospital. Not many people know that an Orpington car was produced in the 1920s, or that Morphy Richards started their electrical business in a local farm in 1936. Some of the finest period architecture in the country can be seen in local district parish churches. The district had many prestigious private schools and currently two of the top achieving grammar schools in the UK. These are only a small list of events and achievements of which Orpington can boast. There are many more and we should be proud of our heritage.

The task of the local historian can be difficult. There has to be a balance between demonstrating one's expertise or understanding of a topic and capturing an audience, and generating interest and interaction. An ongoing challenge for the local historian is to know in which aspects of history individuals are interested in. The author of *Around Orpington Through Time* aspires to cover a very broad range of local interest, relating to the following areas: Orpington, Chelsfield, Crofton, Downe, Farnborough, Green Street Green, Locksbottom, Petts Wood, Pratts Bottom, St Mary Cray and St Paul's Cray. Most of these places were part of the former Orpington Urban District Council and since 1965, they have been part of the London Borough of Bromley. This is not the first book about Orpington, but *Around Orpington Through Time* is the first of its kind for a while, in terms of mainstream publication, to be widely available. It is a pictorial 'then and now' book, and the author hopes it will inform and enable a new generation of people to be interested in their local history. *Around Orpington Through Time* does not propose to give a full-scale history lesson to its readers, but hopes to tempt the reader to look further into Orpington's history via the OHO website after they have closed this book.

To look at our past is to plan our future.

As MP for Orpington, I am proud of my association with the Orpington History Organisation and welcome this book.

Jo Johnson MP

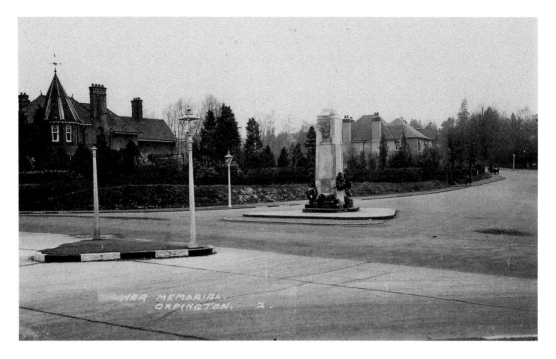

Orpington War Memorial, *c.* 1930

One of Orpington's most iconic landmarks. The war memorial or cenotaph, reminds thousands of residents and passers-by of Orpington's patriotic involvement in conflict at a time when Orpington, as a village, was emerging into the modern era. The memorial was unveiled on Sunday 28 August 1921, designed by Charles Heaton Comyn. The original road junction was just three roads: High Street, Station Hill (later Road) and Sevenoaks Road. The memorial has three lions facing each of the original roads with Spur Road coming later on.

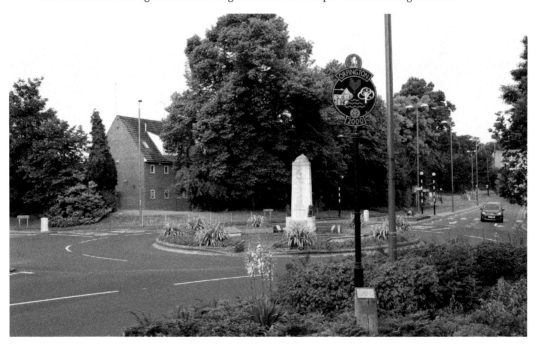

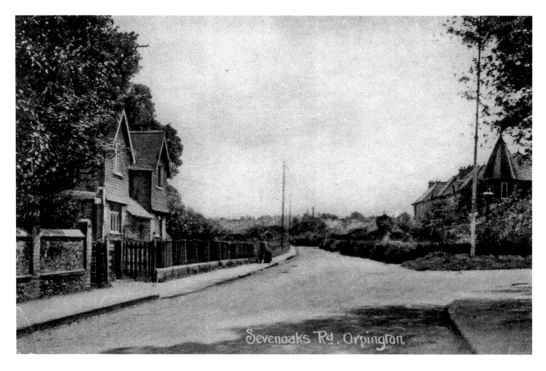

Gravel Pit Cottages, *c.* 1911

An unfamiliar view before the war memorial and roundabout were built. The view here is looking towards Green Street Green. The cottages on the left were part of Gravel Pit Farm and were demolished when Spur Road was constructed, as part of the Orpington Bypass, in 1926. The turreted building ('Corner House') survived until the early 1980s, when it was demolished to make way for Brasted Close.

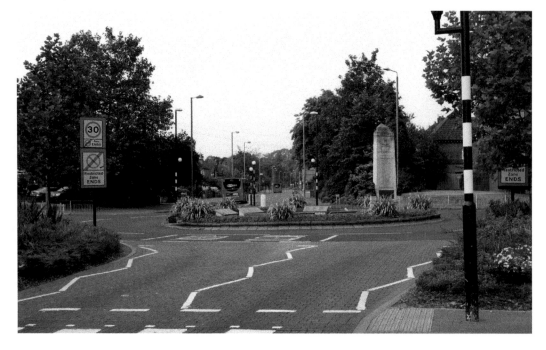

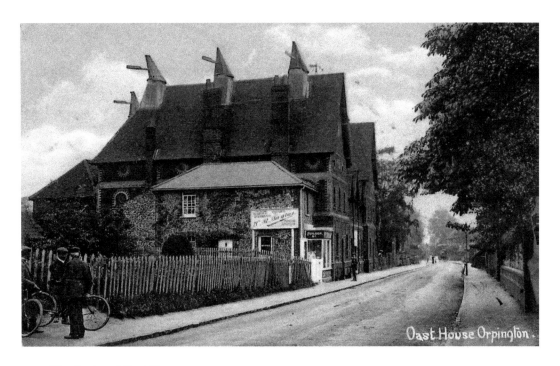

The 'Jackson' Oast House, *c.* 1900

Built in 1866 on what is now the corner of Knoll Rise and the High Street, hops were produced on the Mayfield Estate by the Jackson family (residents of Mayfield Place). At the peak of their production, the farms of Orpington (Mayfield, Perry Hall, Tripes and Court Lodge) were producing an enormous amount of hops and soft fruit. In the late 1800s, it is claimed that soft fruit production from Mayfield was among the highest in Britain for many years. The oast house was demolished in 1924 and the corner of Knoll Rise was developed.

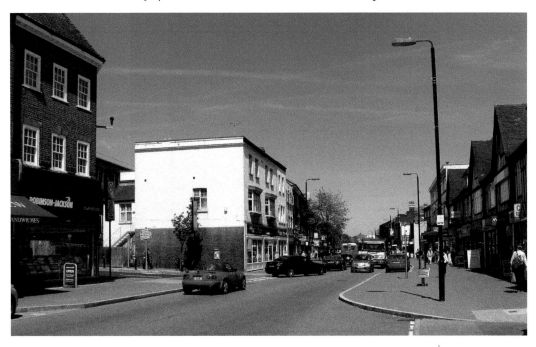

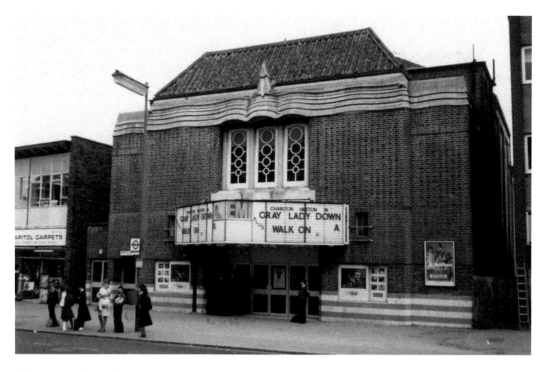

The Commodore Cinema, 1978

Many different establishments provided entertainment in the town, but for years the Commodore Cinema was the preferred venue to watch the latest newsreels and films. Built and opened in 1933 by the Spencer-May family, the cinema was another local landmark. Built with considerable internal and external art deco features, the cinema closed in 1982 and was later demolished after a fire. The cinema will once again return to Orpington, as a development of a new Odeon branded multiscreen complex in the Walnuts Shopping Centre is well on its way.

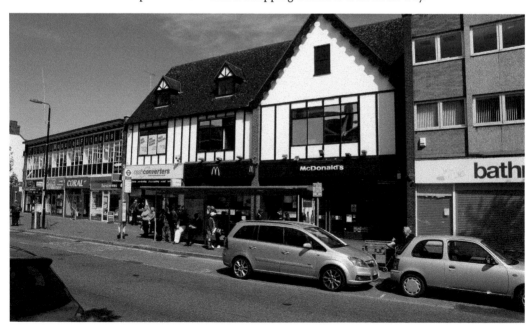

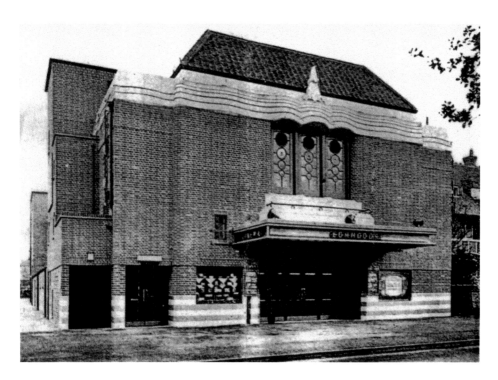

The Commodore Cinema, Late 1930s

As you can see from the images on this page, the cinema was an impressive looking place in 1930s Orpington and the Art Deco interior as seen in the late 1960s was pleasantly adorned with the 'Christie' organ centre stage. This organ was saved and is being carefully restored by Christie theatre organ enthusiast Chris Cartwright. (*Above: Philip Lane. Below: Chris Cartwright*)

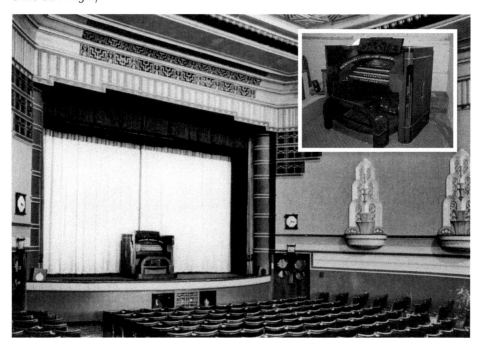

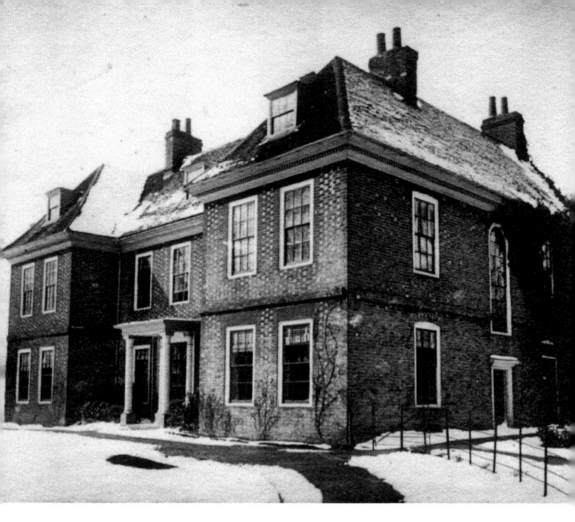

Mayfield Place, *c.* 1920

Mayfield Place stood magnificently at the centre of the Manor of Mayfield, or Little Orpington, for many years. Built in 1750, it survived into the 1930s, well after the Mayfield Estate, Farm and title of Lord of the Manor ceased to exist. A campaign to keep it for use as a municipal building gave way to pressure to develop the High Street for the expanding population of Orpington. Want to learn more about the manor? *History on our Doorstep* by the residents of Vinson Close is available for purchase at Orpington Library. (*Bromley Local Studies Department*)

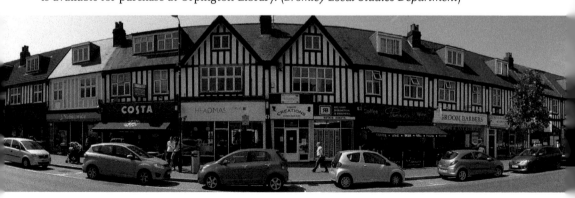

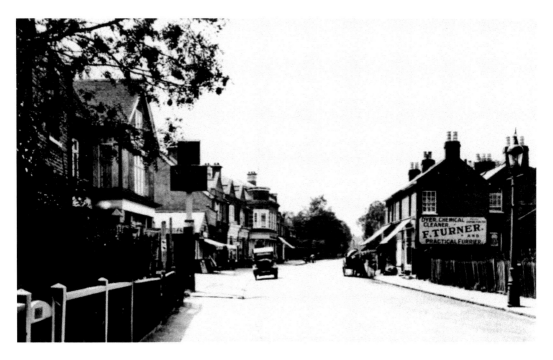

Orpington High Street, Coach and Horses, *c.* 1920

This view has changed significantly since it was taken in 1920. We are looking south along the High Street with Homefield Rise on the left. The only building recognisable here now is the NatWest Bank premises on the corner. The word 'home' was typically applied to 'farm' or 'field' where a large residence, such as a manor house, had its own farm. The land on which Homefield Rise and its housing estate was developed originally belonged to Gravel Pit and Court Lodge farms, which have long since disappeared.

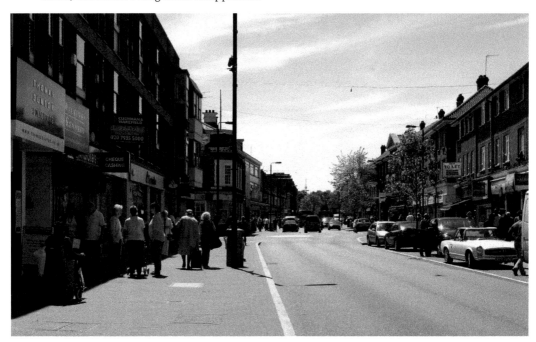

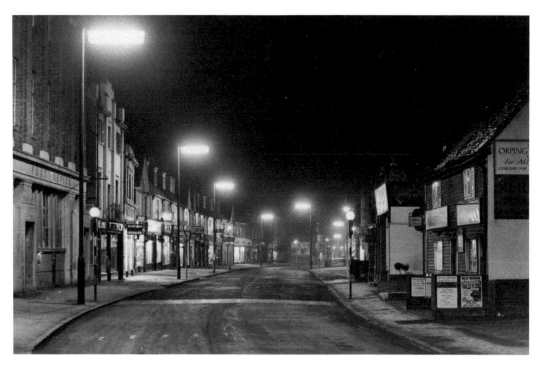

Orpington High Street, New Street Lighting, 1954
Orpington's first modern set of street lights, recorded by a forward-thinking council employee who took a number of these images the evening they were switched on. These images show some older buildings still in place. The post office is instantly recognisable. The building that used to house the former Woolworths had not yet been built, and the Walnuts Shopping Centre entrance and buildings were just designs on a drawing board! (*Bromley Local Studies Department*)

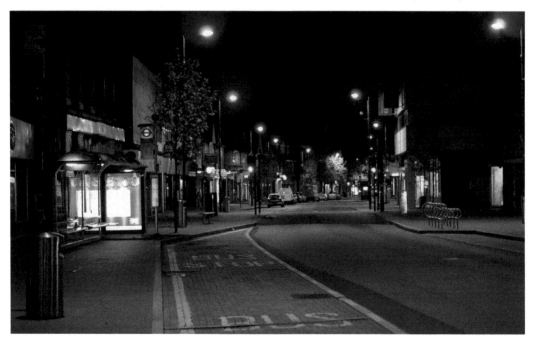

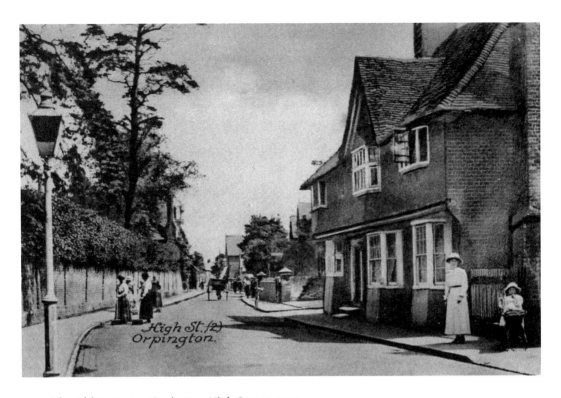

The Old Cottages, Orpington High Street, 1914

Believe it or not, these two cottages were some of the oldest existing buildings in Orpington, going back to the early seventeenth century. They were located close to the previous image. The wall to the left was that of Mayfield Place. You may be surprised to know that they were demolished in 1938 in the name of progress! If they had survived to this period, they would surely have been a cherished attraction to the High Street. (*Jean Bodfish Collection*)

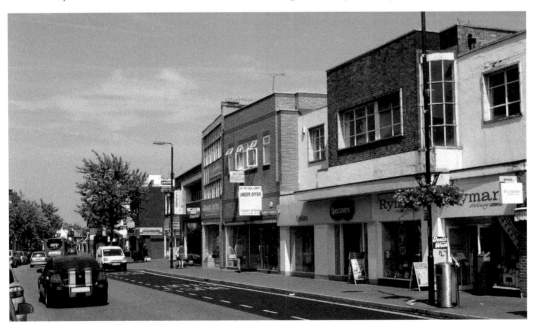

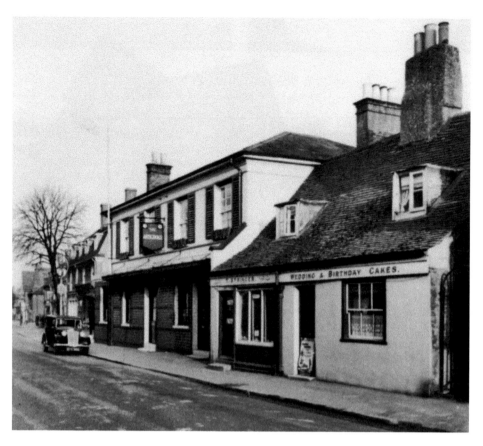

The Artichoke Public House, 1939

Orpington had many public houses, inns and associated hotels. Many of them survive. Here is the Artichoke, built around 1855. It existed with the White Hart, the Change of Horses, the Cricketers and the Anchor and Hope for years. Each offered something slightly different for their clientele. Today, the building still stands as a successful Turkish restaurant. (*Bromley Local Studies Department*)

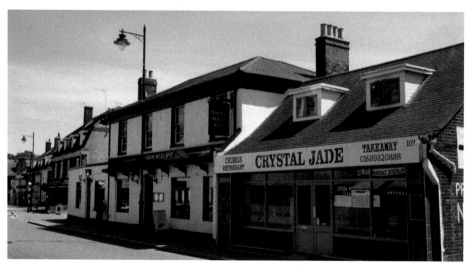

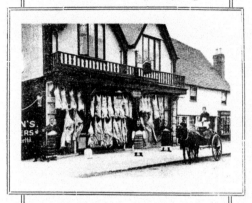

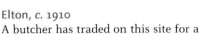

E. J. Elton
Butcher & Grazier,
Aberdeen House, Orpington

MR. E. J. ELTON begs to inform his patrons and the neighbourhood generally that he is in a position to supply **choicest Scotch & English Beef, Mutton & Lamb**, also the best brands of **Canterbury Mutton & Lamb**, at prices which, compared with those of the leading stores and firms, will effect a **Material Saving**. Should a change of tradesmen be under consideration, Mr. E. J. ELTON respectfully ———— solicits a trial. ————

Elton, *c.* 1910

A butcher has traded on this site for a very long time. Mr Edward Elton and his family business were notable in the village and later town. Aberdeen House is the correct name for the building that contains the shop and former dwellings. As they became more prosperous, the Eltons moved into a large house just back from the High Street called Drayton Lodge, which was purchased by the London Borough of Bromley and demolished to make way for the Walnuts Shopping Centre. Elton's started trading from Aberdeen House around 1907 and, as you can see, Majestic Catering are continuing the tradition today.

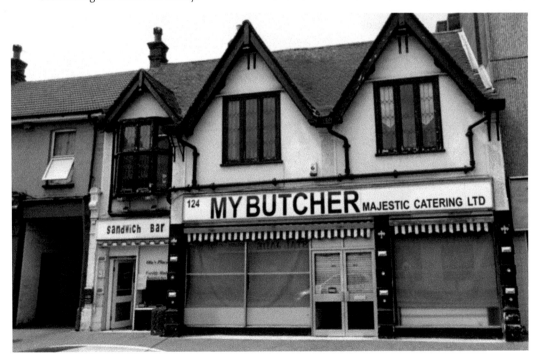

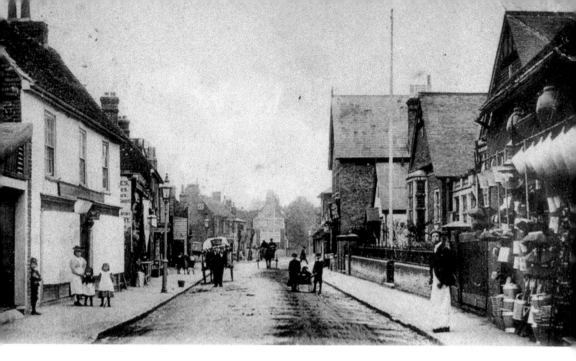

The High Street and Village Hall, *c.* 1903
Designed by George St Pierre Harris and given to the villagers in 1890 by the late Alfred Brown Esq, the village hall and social club (*seen to the right*) were central to the village. The hall hosted numerous events, including weddings, exhibitions, formal meetings and social events, until a serious fire devastated the building in 1961. The social club (previous home of the Liberal Club) survived until the early 1980s when it, and the derelict village hall, were flattened and the modern Templegate complex was built.

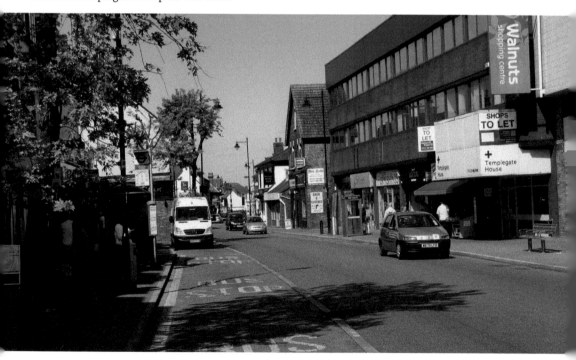

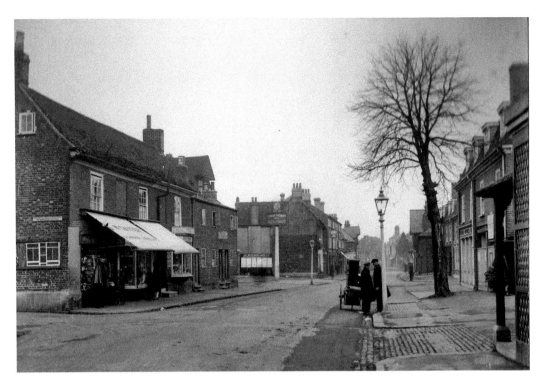

D. W. Gayfer, Town Watch, Clockmaker and Jeweller, 1927

A High Street view showing the premises Mr D. W. Gayfer occupied (No. 112 High Street) on the corner of Broomhill Road. Many will associate this shop with the Sweet Shop, which traded there for most of the twentieth century. At the time of this picture, the Sweet Shop was actually next door at No. 114 High Street. Mr Gayfer developed two shops and upper floor residences on the corner of White Hart Road and in 1929, moved in. Mr Gayfer traded for nearly forty years, selling the business and property to Mr King in 1937. (*Above: Frank Evans Collection*)

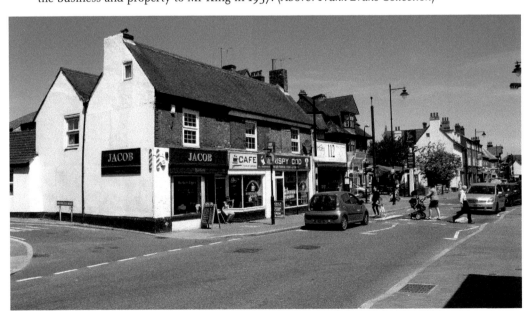

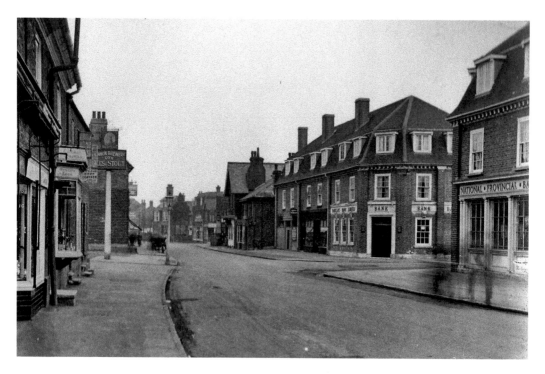

High Street and Church Hill, 1927

This image shows the two 'new' Bank buildings on both corners of Church Hill. Barclays Bank occupied the north side and the Provincial Bank the south. The upper floor of the Provincial Bank was also a school for a while. Interestingly, the village stocks and gibbet stood on the corner occupied by the Barclays Bank for hundreds of years. This was when laws in Orpington, as in other parishes and manors, were enforced locally with justice and punishment. (*Above: Frank Evans Collection*)

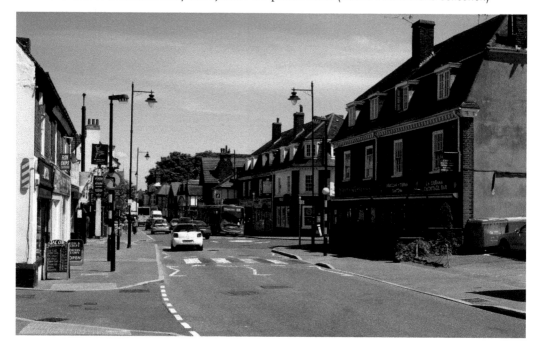

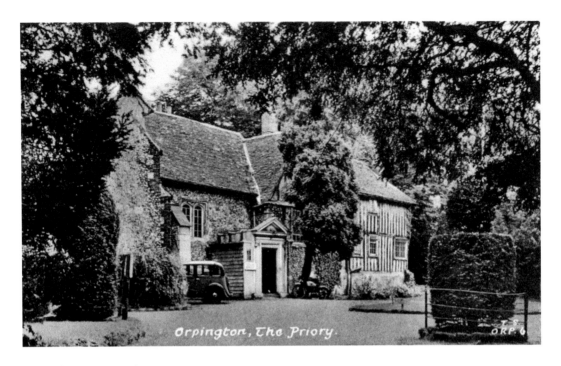

Orpington, The Priory.

The Priory, Orpington, c. 1930

The Priory, which stands on a former Saxon estate, can be traced back to the late thirteenth century. The priory was an important stop off and Orpington's rectory for many years. At its core, the priory is a medieval hall house. Considerable thirteenth-, fourteenth- and fifteenth-century architecture is clearly visible with many impressive interior Tudor examples. The Bromley Museum, which is based at the priory, offers free admission to displays relating to the Borough and its past. In the modern-day image, from right to left, is the current Museum Curator Ms Marie-Louise Kerr, and Cultural Business Development Officer, Ms Kay Coulton.

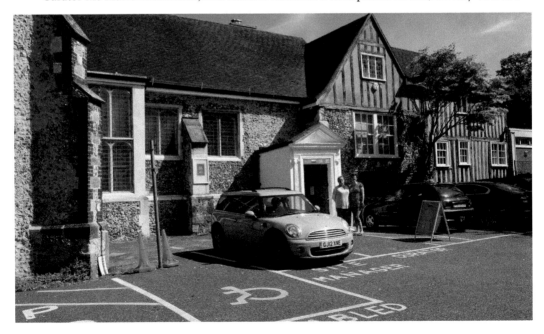

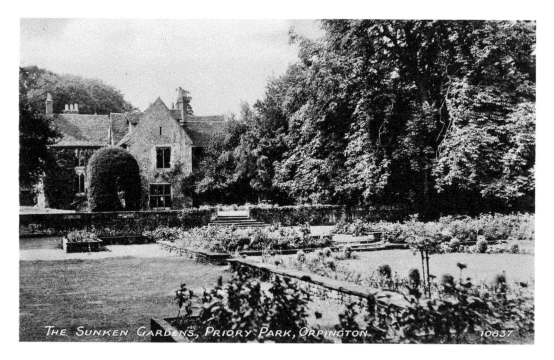

The Sunken Gardens, the Priory, Orpington, 1964

The Priory Gardens, now a public recreational space, were once the private gardens of the priory house and date from the seventeenth century. The last private residents of the priory, the Hughes family, made many improvements to the gardens, including the rose gardens and sunken garden. Today, the garden is listed by English Heritage as Grade II. The vast majority of the features added by the Hughes still exist today and, along with the ponds, children's play park and walking areas, make the Priory Gardens a very popular recreational space for the town.

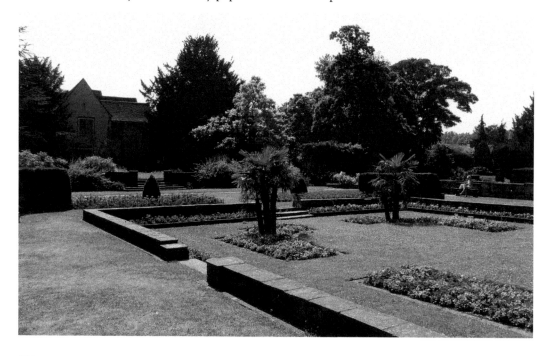

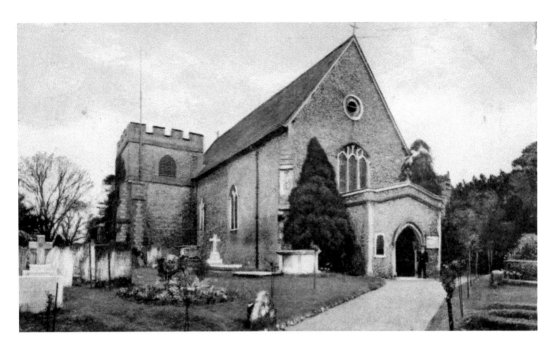

All Saints Church, 1909

The parish church of All Saints, Orpington, is the oldest existing building in Orpington. The church has been present on this site for over 1000 years, standing on pre-Norman foundations. Mentioned in the Domesday Book, some Saxon parts of the church are still visible along with a sundial. All Saints had a spire that was destroyed by lightning strikes twice! In 1957, the church was significantly extended using land gained by the demolition of Bark Hart House. The church is located on a slight hill above Orpington High Street, where an old riverbed is located and would occasionally flood. (*Above: Lynn Sculpher Collection*)

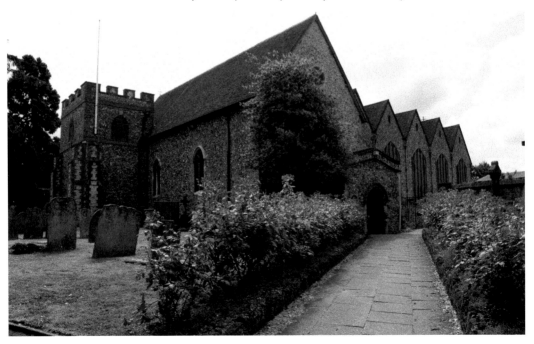

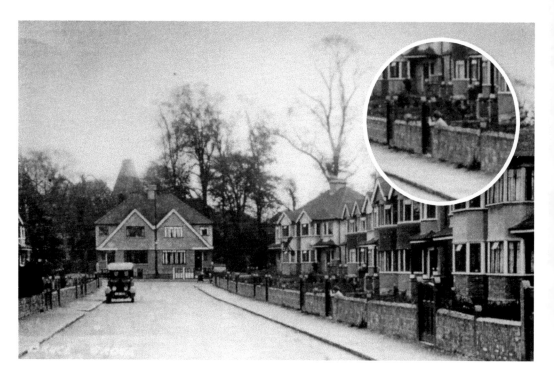

Bruce Grove, 1933

This road was built on land purchased from the nearby Court Lodge Farm (the farm's oast house is in the background) by Mr C. L. 'Lenny' Bruce, who was an entrepreneur of the town. The little boy (*enlarged in the inset*) in the old postcard is a very young Master Frank Evans, who is the grandson of D. W. Gayfer, town jeweller. The man in the modern-day photograph is the one and the same Mr Frank Evans, who is eighty-six years young and an inspiration to us all!

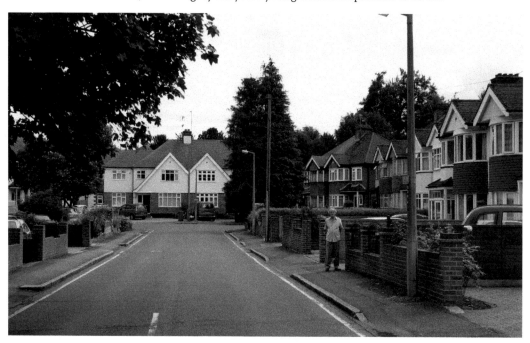

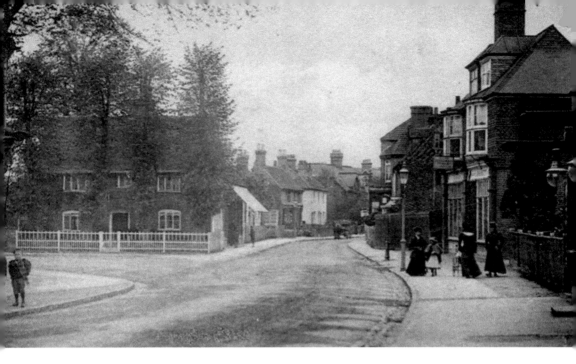

Rose Cottage and the Junction of Chislehurst Road, *c.* 1905
This is the junction of the High Street and Chislehurst Road, which in those days was the main road junction into and out of the village. On the north corner is the Limes or Rose Cottages, which were built in 1690 and for centuries would have been well known and instantly recognisable. Popplewells was a drapers shop at the back of the Limes, established by Mr John Popplewell, son of Joseph, the principal teacher at the British School. The Limes and what was left of Popplewell's shop became run down and were demolished in the 1970s.

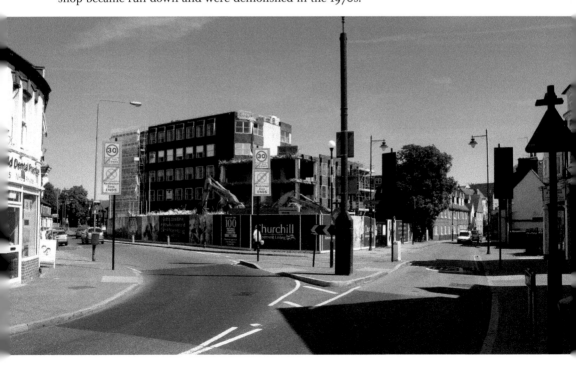

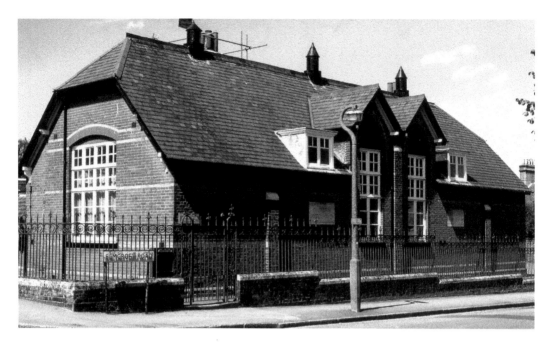

Chislehurst Road School, 1985

Before 1870, children only went to school if their parents could afford it or a wealthy benefactor provided the education. Education boards were established under the 1870 Education Act as part of the local authority changes in Victorian Britain. The board existed to ensure that education was available to all. The 'Board School', Chislehurst Road, was built in 1882 and extended in 1897 and was Orpington's first purpose-built school for all. (*Above: Colin Churcher*)

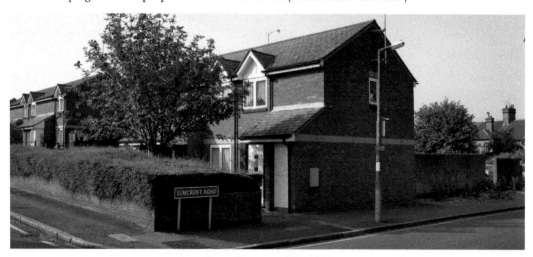

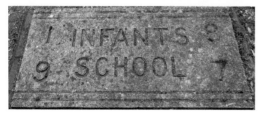

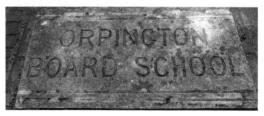

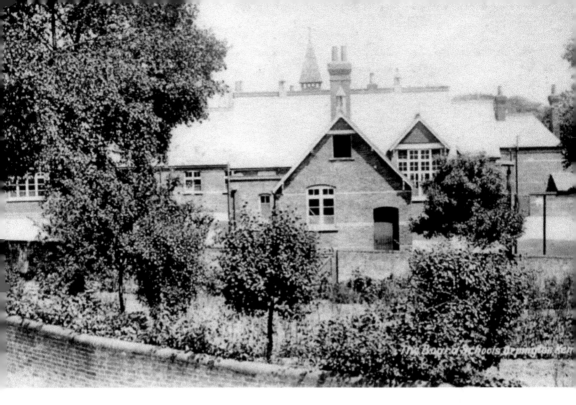

The Board School, *c.* 1900

Typically, infant schools segregated girls from boys. The early syllabus was the 'three Rs': Reading, wRiting and aRithmetic. Religion would also play a role, typically through Bible reading and hymn singing. School boards were abolished in 1902. Chislehurst Road School educated many local children and finally closed its doors in the very late 1980s. The old infants' school building at Chislehurst Road was demolished and developed for housing. The main school buildings are now private residences and are also used by the Local Health Authority.

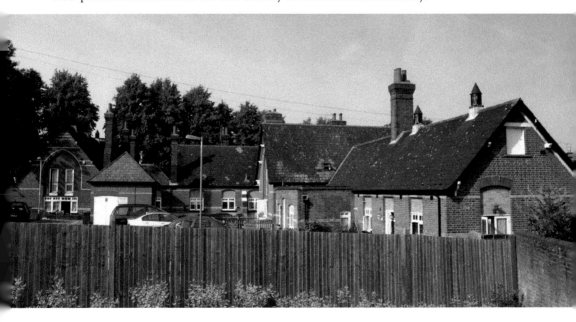

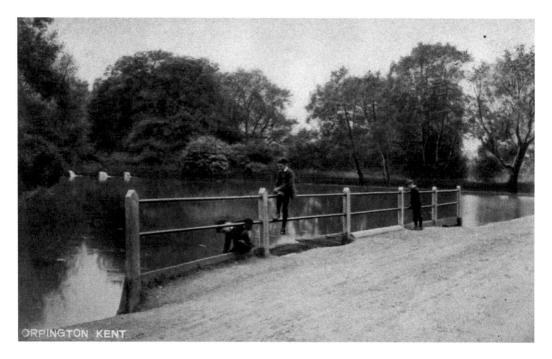

The Priory Ponds, *c.* 1910

The Priory ponds are the head and source of the River Cray. In years gone by, the ponds have had many uses. They were used to water livestock, fill bowsers for drinking water and for steam engines to take on water. In addition, water would power a number of large mills further down the river. Today, the ponds are the home of a healthy number of waterfowl. In the above image, the boys are possibly fishing for sticklebacks where the water flows under the road to become the River Cray.

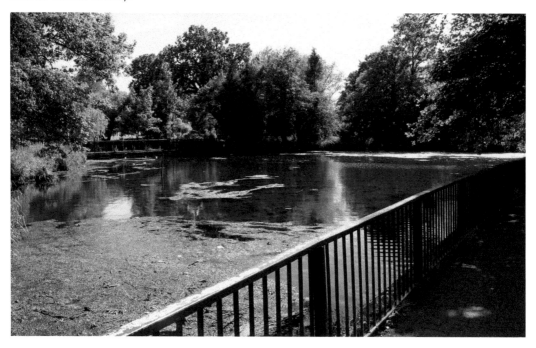

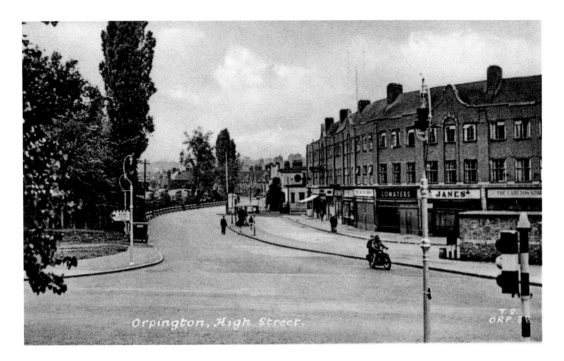

Carlton Parade, c. 1950

The current 1920s shopping parade has a hidden history. Less than 100 years ago, this area was still very rural. The land of a large Corn Mill existed on the current site of Carlton Parade and the residential housing behind it. The mill was the first on the River Cray and had its own header ponds to maintain the power for the waterwheel. The parade of shops was also the location of the old former Palace Cinema and Smith and Millroy's workshops, where they built the Orpington Car.

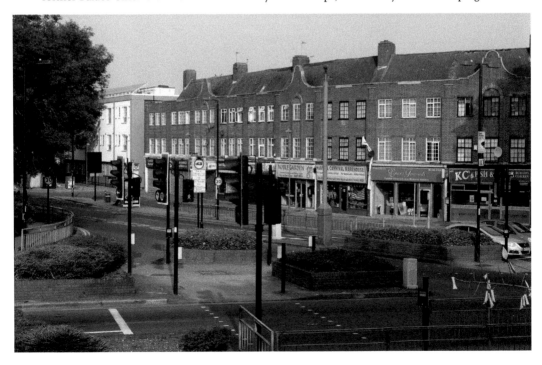

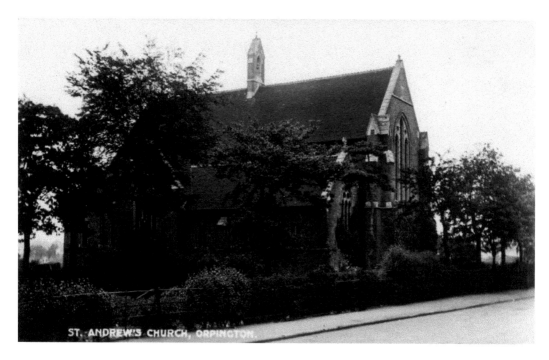

ST. ANDREW'S CHURCH, ORPINGTON.

St Andrews Church, *c.* 1930

St Andrews was built and opened in 1893 on Lower Road to support the stretched-to-capacity parish church of All Saints, Orpington. St Andrews initially took its congregation from the residents of New Town. However, the next wave of development was taking place to the north-east of Orpington on the former land of Northfield Hall, and St Andrews' congregation boomed. Although St Andrews started as an extension of All Saints, it became a parish church in its own right in 1935.

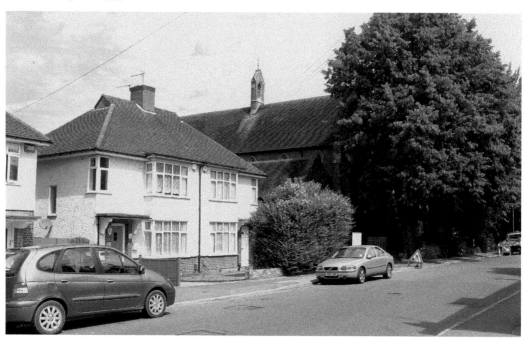

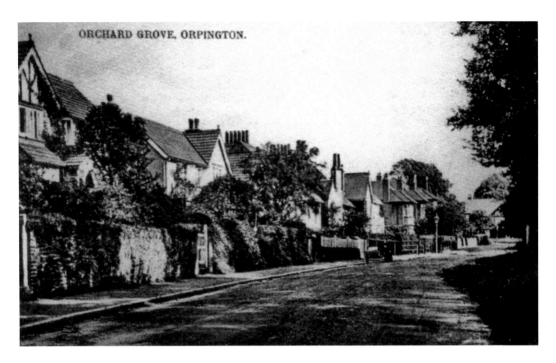

ORCHARD GROVE, ORPINGTON.

Orchard Grove, *c.* 1923

The Edwardian houses built here were inconspicuous for nearly a century, until they became a controversial part of the redevelopment of the former Station Road car park in the mid-2000s. Virtually unchanged since their construction, this line of detached dwellings, with significant rear gardens, would all (but one) disappear during the spring of 2008. The residents formerly objected to the proposed development, but ultimately planning was finally granted and they had to sell their properties. The appearance of Orchard Grove changed forever.

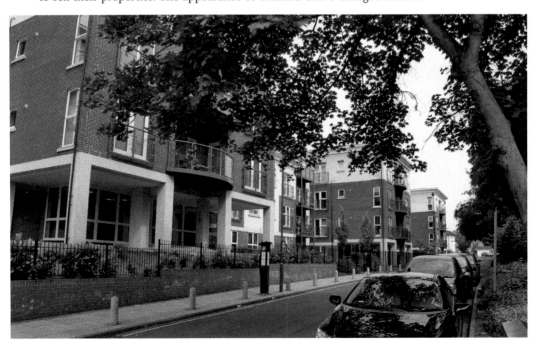

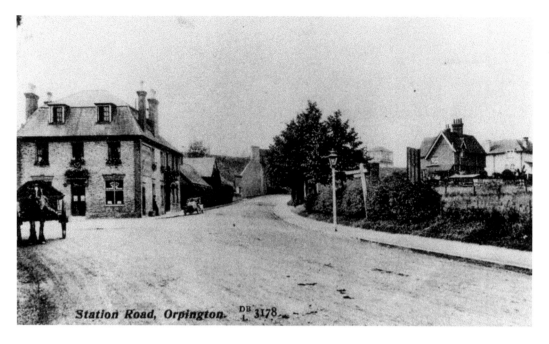

Station Road, the Maxwell Arms/Hotel, *c.* 1910

The railway came to Orpington in 1868. At that time, Orpington was a sleepy village surrounded by typical Kent farms producing hops, soft fruit and livestock. The railway would change Orpington forever. Most railway stations were accompanied by public houses, and so the Maxwell Arms was built in 1887. The name comes from one of the last families that resided at Tubbenden House, which was located approximately where Shelley Close is today. (*Above: Bromley Local Studies Department*)

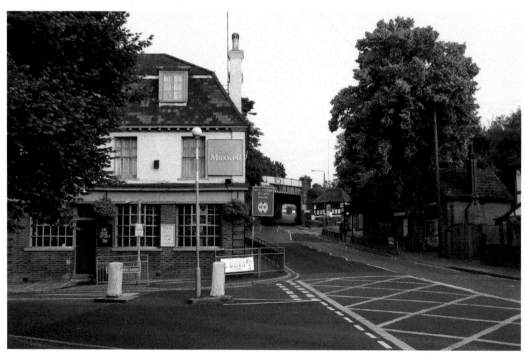

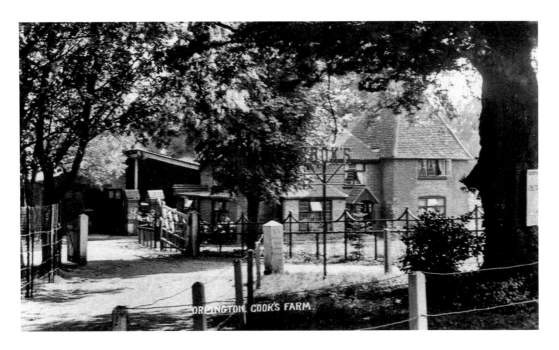

William Henry Cook, Tubbenden Lane, *c.* 1930

'Billie', or 'W. H.', became William Cook & Sons' General Manager at Orpington House, Walden's Farm, St Mary Cray, where they produced the famous Orpington chickens and ducks. W. H. split from his father and by 1904 was trading his own poultry business at 'The Model Poultry Farm', Gray's Farm in St Paul's Cray. In 1912, W.H. moved his business to the grounds of Tubbenden House. When W.H. retired in 1947, the business was sold and by the early 1950s the farmland was all houses. Dalton Close was built in the 1960s on the site of the Lodge House where W.H. lived. The mile marker can still be seen today; it reads 'XV Miles to London Bridge 1779'.

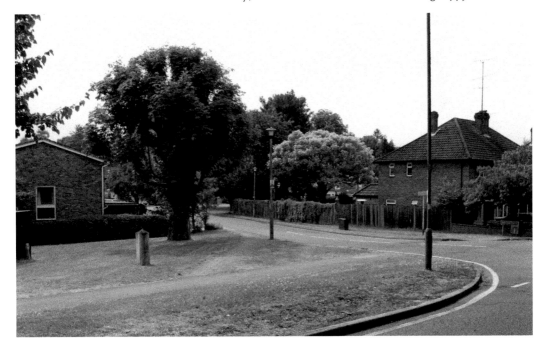

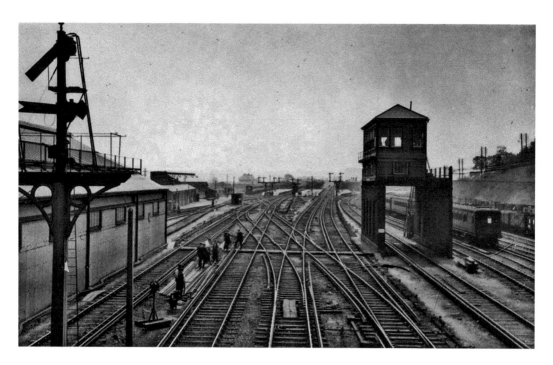

Orpington Railway Station, 1927

Orpington station was opened on 2 March 1868, when the South Eastern Railway (SER) opened its line between Chislehurst and Tonbridge. The station is the main reason why Orpington expanded from a medium-sized village to a prosperous expanding town in just over fifty years, and is why some of the suburbs of Orpington are well established although not even 100 years old. Today, Orpington station serves three West End and four City of London stations with 5 million passenger journeys a year!

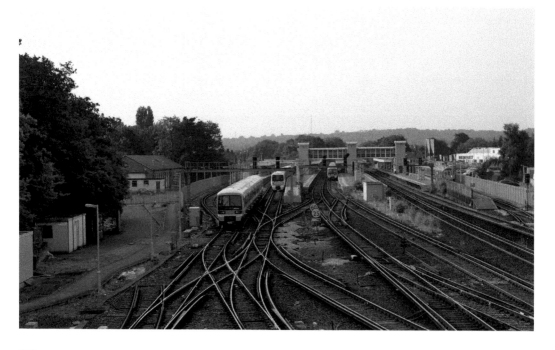

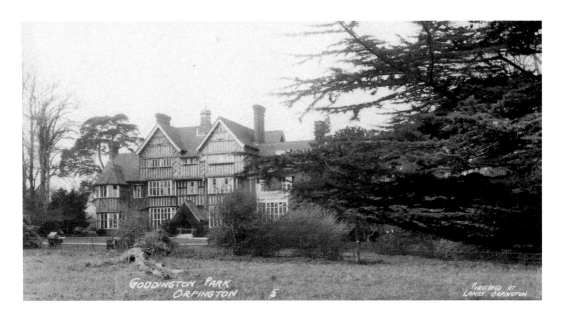

Goddington House, *c.* 1920

Goddington Manor house was extensively remodelled in 1893 by William West Neve for Alexander Miller Hallett. The large estate was sold piecemeal between 1919 and 1931; Spur Road and the Orpington Bypass were driven through the park, and housing estates built on it, though much parkland was acquired by Orpington Council in 1934. In 1982, the house was left to the Methodist Ministers' Housing Society. It was recently sold to developers who have retained and restored the attractive Arts and Crafts features (*see inset*). (*Above: Bill Morton. Below: Geoffrey Copus*)

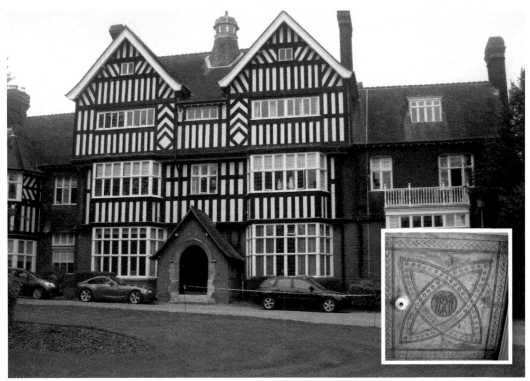

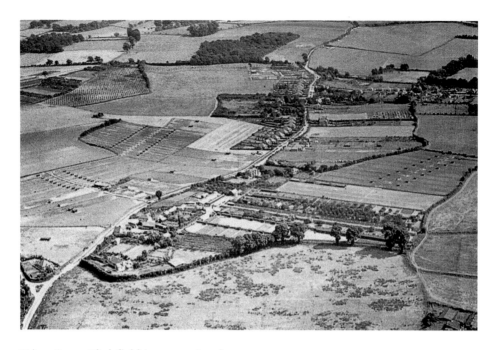

Tripes Farm, Chelsfield Lane, 1936 and *c.* 2000
This is Tripes Farm and Chelsfield Lane in 1930. You can see how big it was! It was famous for its sausages and poultry. The original farm buildings are over 400 years old. You will notice that Ramsden Estate is still Ramsden Farm (*very bottom of picture*) and Tripes Farm was formerly located on what is now Alma Road, Loxwood Close, Moyser Drive and Gload Crescent. Mr C. George Senior of Tripes built houses on and widened Chelsfield Lane in the 1920s, and those houses are still there today. (*Above: Charles George*)

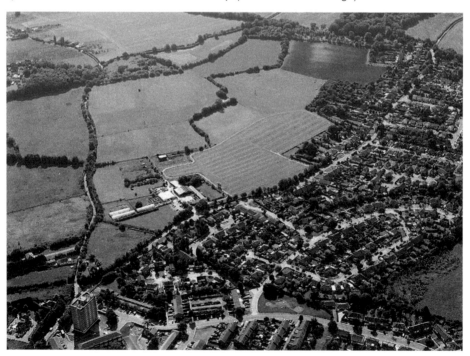

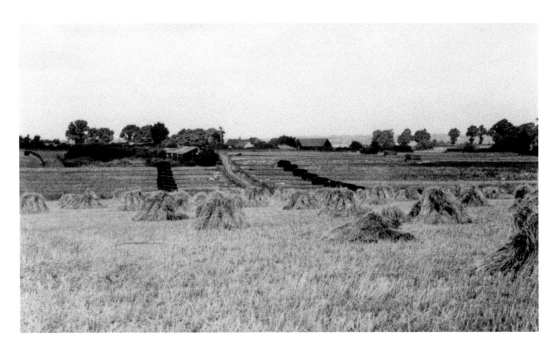

Tripes Farm, Chelsfield Lane, 1930 and c. 2000

Tripes Farm once formed part of the Manor of Mayfield within the Manor of Orpington. The oldest remaining buildings on Tripes Farm date from 1540 (Tudor). 'Tripes' is the only remaining farm in the Parish of Orpington. 'Tripes' was a very large working farm in the early part of the twentieth century. The current farm has been worked by the George family since 1911 and once boasted the largest outdoor pig production enterprise in the UK. The farm is well known today for its commercial centre and its very popular car boot sales held fourteen times each year. (*Above: Charles George*)

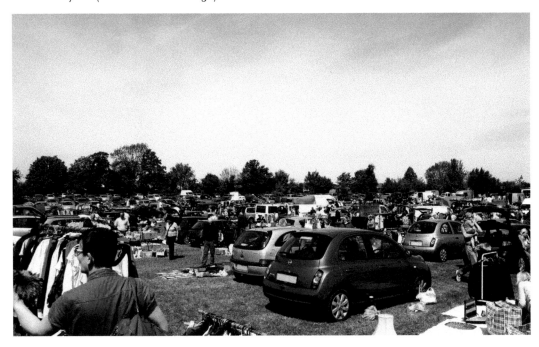

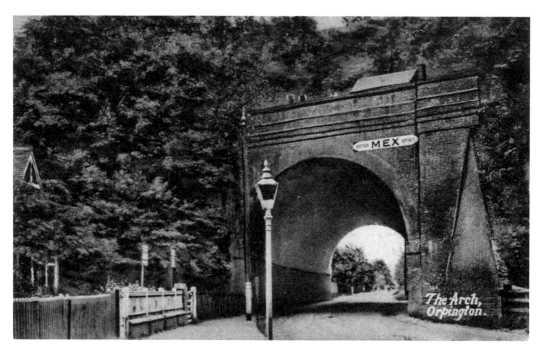

Boundary Garage and South Eastern Railway 'Triumph Arch', c. 1920

The Boundary estate existed long before the railway sliced through it in 1868, and was so named because the estate and farm sat on the boundary between Orpington and Green Street Green. In later years, the owners of the boundary estate gave a huge amount of land to the Ontario government, which became Orpington Hospital. Boundary Garage can be seen here on the left, with the South Eastern Railway's 'Triumph Arch' spanning the main road from Orpington to Green Street Green (Sevenoaks Road). At the time, it was the largest hand-built brick-road tunnel in the south.

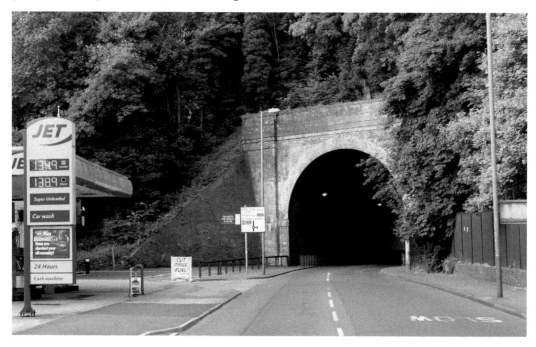

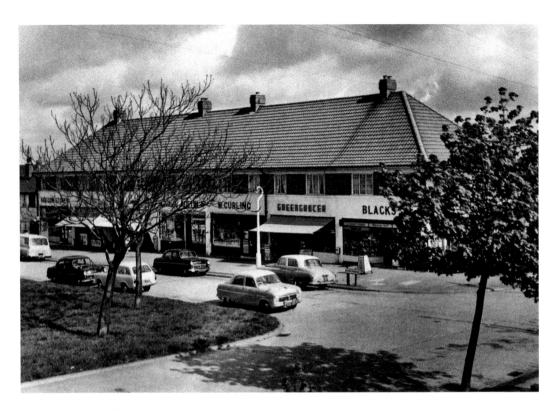

Kelvin Parade, *c.* 1955

Kelvin Parade, just west of Orpington railway station, is situated in one of the many 1920s and 1930s housing estates that sprung up on former estates and farmland in the district. The parade, as seen in the earlier photograph, was typical of similar parades and would have boasted a baker, butcher, greengrocer, post office, general store and newsagent/confectioner/tobacconist. In fact, Blacks, as seen in the image, is fondly remembered by many of the Orpington History Organisation's members as where they would spend their childhood pocket money! Kelvin Parade was also the terminus of the 477 bus.

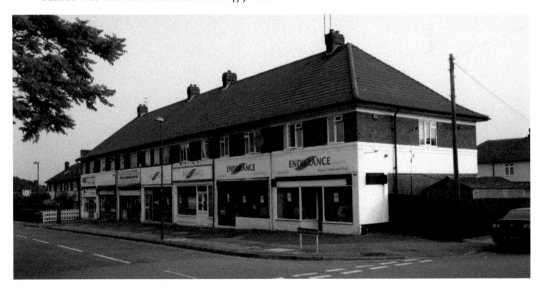

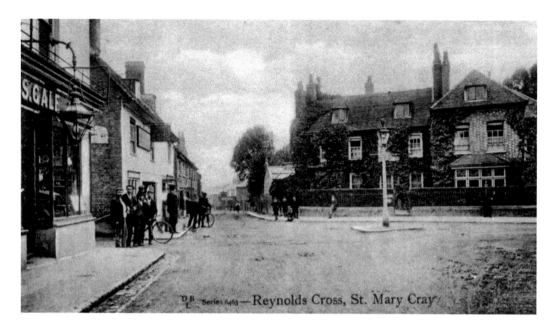

DB Series 6463 — Reynolds Cross, St. Mary Cray

Reynolds Cross, *c.* 1900
This was the main junction with St Mary Cray High Street. It has been known as Reynolds Cross, after Reynold Smith who had a nearby smallholding for well over 100 years. Coaches left here daily at 8 a.m. for Greenwich and the London and Greenwich Railway, which was the district's nearest rail link to the city. Many photographs were taken of this place for postcards and almost all of them have a policeman from the local St Mary Cray Police directing traffic. Until the bypass was built, this was a very busy junction.

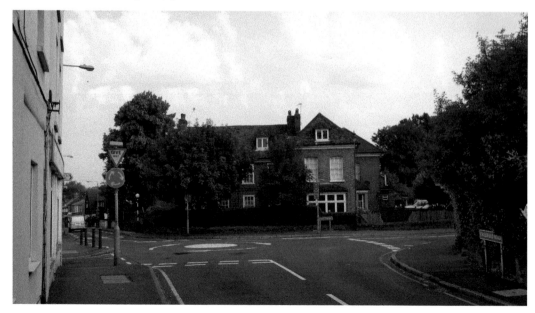

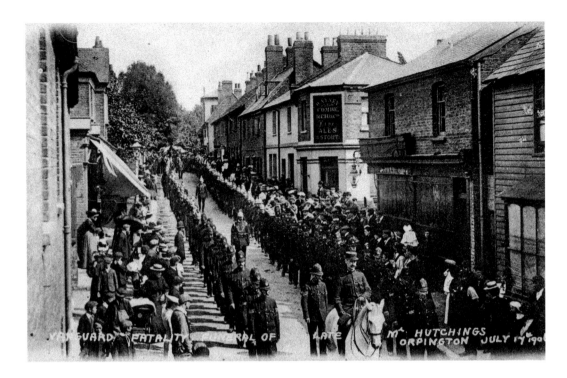

Vanguard Bus Disaster, *c.* 1906

A tragic end to a trip to Brighton for members and friends of the Crays and Orpington Volunteer Fire Brigades. Just before 11 a.m. on Thursday 12 July, the brakes of the hired Vanguard bus failed on the steep descent to the village of Handcross in Sussex. Ten were killed, six instantly, including Henry Hutchings, an undertaker. The funerals, held over three days, attracted huge gatherings and 3,000 attended that of Mr Hutchings. This postcard shows his cortège leaving St Mary Cray for All Saints' church in Orpington. This was the world's first bus disaster and is now just a footnote in history books and a regularly mistitled postcard on eBay.

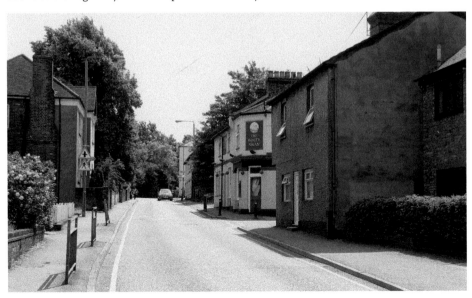

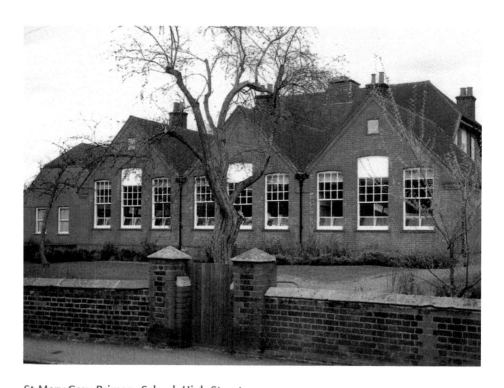

St Mary Cray Primary School, High Street, *c.* 1995
This is the 1909 building that, at the time, replaced an older building. This possibly links back to the very first school in St Mary Cray or Orpington, called the St Mary Cray Charity School of 1816. The outer wall of the former school is still in place. As with Chislehurst Road School in Orpington, this was St Mary Cray's Education Board School. (*Above: Lynn Sculpher Collection*)

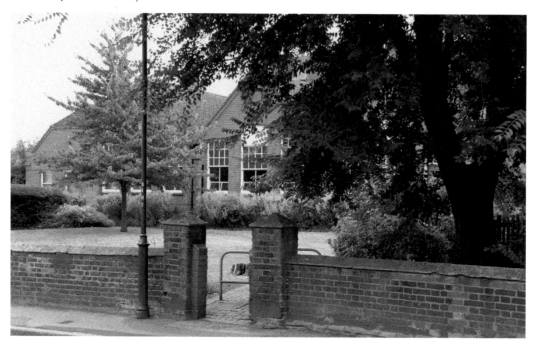

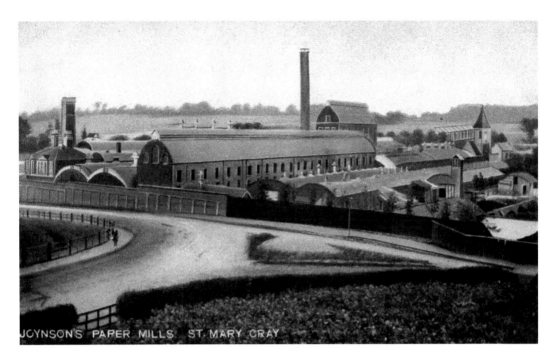

JOYNSON'S PAPER MILLS ST MARY CRAY

Joynson's Paper Mill, *c.* 1911
This is Joynson's Paper Mill in St Mary Cray. This huge mill was located where modern large retailers trade their wares today (on the north side of the railway embankment). Joynson's produced high quality paper and banknote paper. The mill closed in 1967 and was then demolished. It was a significant employer in the area and the chimney alone could be seen from a long way away.

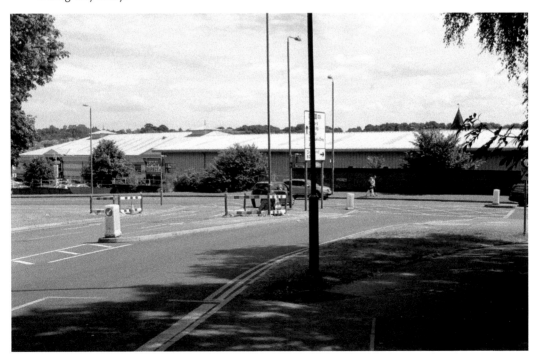

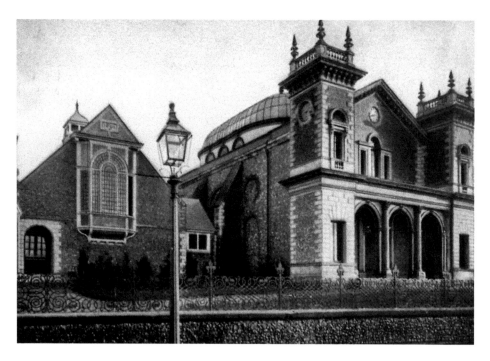

St Mary Cray, Original Temple Church and Moffat Hall, *c.* 1900
The Temple United Reformed church has been part of the community of St Mary Cray for well over 150 years. It was William Joynson of Joynson's Paper Mill who contributed a huge amount of money to build the church (built 1851) and Moffat Hall (built 1891). The former main church building was hit by a parachuted landmine in 1941 and the structure irreparably damaged. By 1950, it was considered unsafe and had to close. A new church was built and reopened in 1955, and it continues to serve the community to this day. (*Above: Lynn Sculpher Collection*)

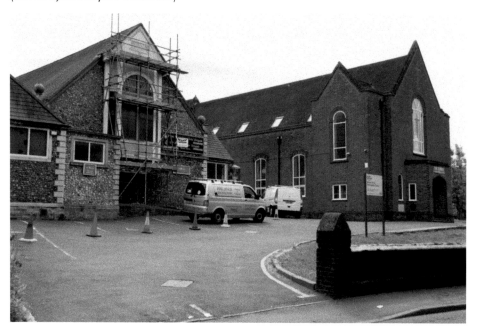

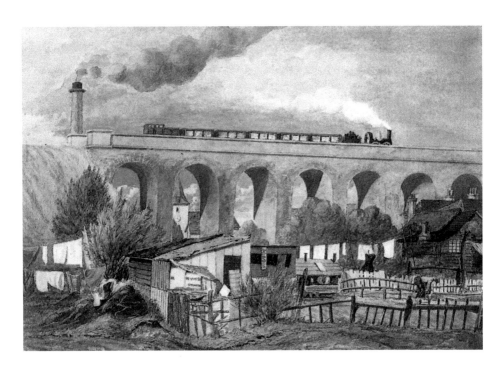

Artist's Illustration of St Mary Cray Railway Viaduct, c. 1860
As mentioned in other parts of this book, the railway expanse of the mid- and late nineteenth century would change the area forever. St Mary Cray was reached by the London Chatham and Dover Railway in 1860. This would have been a remarkable spectacle for the people of St Mary Cray. Unlike Orpington, the line was built right across the centre of the parish and town. The nineteenth-century view depicted by the postcard would have initially appeared to have been something out of science fiction for the rural residents! (*Above: Lynn Sculpher Collection*)

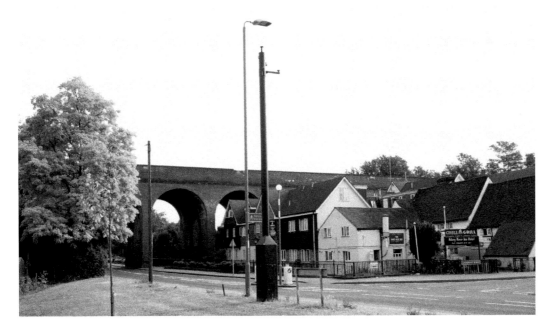

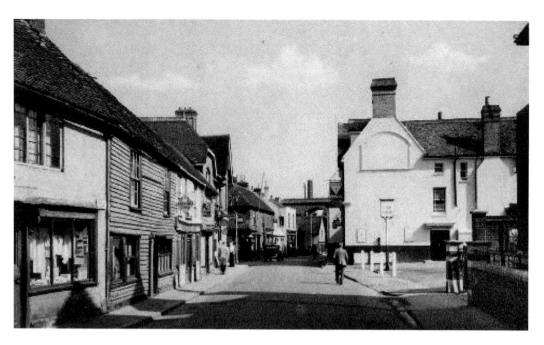

St Mary Cray High Street, Looking North, *c.* 1950

A view looking north along St Mary Cray High Street. Many older buildings still remain, but sadly some do not. Traffic has been diverted from this side of the viaduct (as it has the north side), giving a very subdued existence, which is in complete contrast to how things would have been 100 years ago. You have to imagine a time when St Mary Cray was the market town of the district – it had industry in mills and foundries, and was reached by the railway before Orpington.

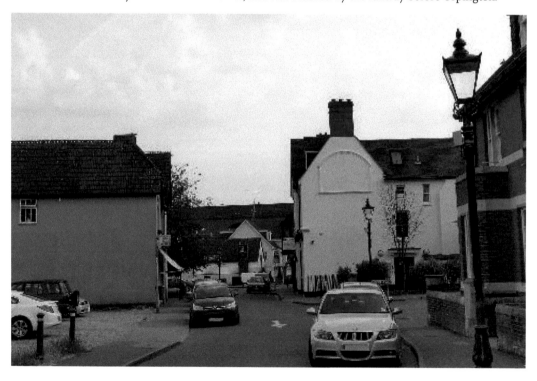

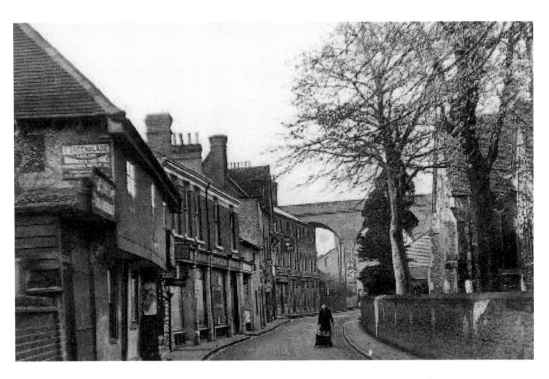

St Mary Cray High Street, Looking South, *c.* 1900
They say a picture paints a thousand words and this applies to this one! The buildings to the left are very old and still remain today. The parish church is to the right. Today, each side of the original St Mary Cray High Street is a cul-de-sac. In the days when this old photograph was taken, the High Street was a very busy thoroughfare. (*Below: Trevor Hayman*)

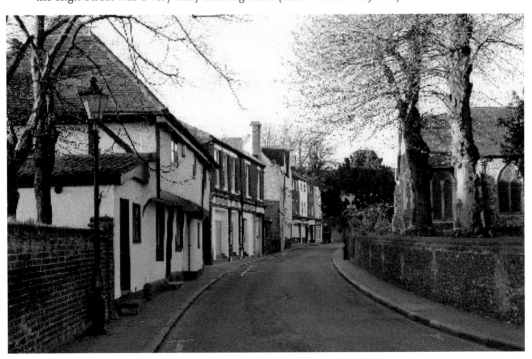

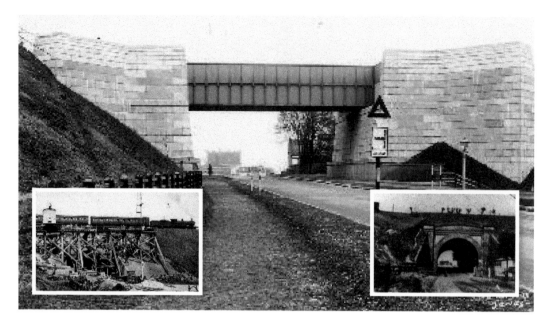

St Mary Cray Railway Bridge, c. 1910, c. 1925 and c. 1930
In the 1920s, the need for arterial roads and bypasses became a necessity and the Orpington Bypass, constructed by local civil engineering company Fordyce Brothers in 1926, stretched from St Paul's Cray all the way south to Badgers Mount. At St Mary Cray, there was one significant obstacle to overcome and that was to remove the older 1860 tunnel, which gave passage to a small local road, and put in place a wider bridge to span the new A224 bypass. (*Above: Bromley Local Studies Department*)

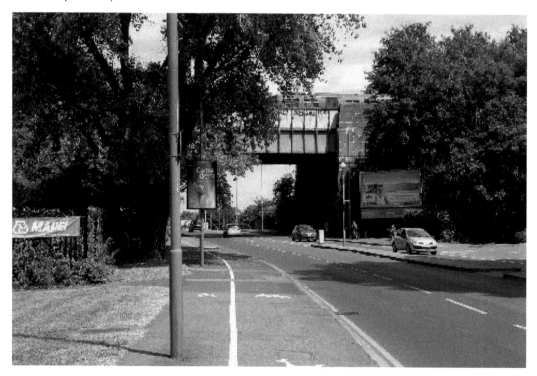

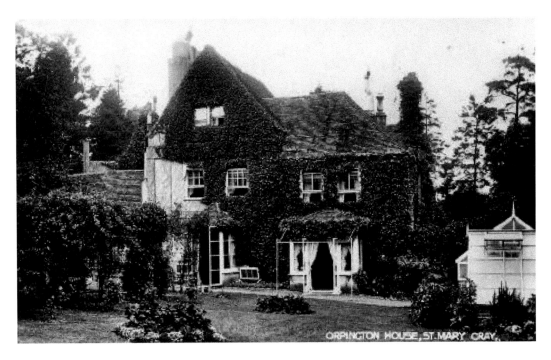

Orpington House, Now Walden's Manor, St Mary Cray, c. 1910
William Cook Senior bought Walden's Manor and its farm in 1889, moving from Tower House, Sevenoaks Road, Orpington. William renamed the manor house Orpington House, and this would be the address of the business until 1934. William created the Orpington chicken in 1886. William developed various colours of the chicken and Orpington duck and one of the highlights was that the Jubilee Orpington chicken was presented to Queen Victoria for her Diamond Jubilee. After a long international trip in 1904, William returned to England and, suffering from chronic emphysema, sadly died on 25 June at the age of fifty-five. Elizabeth Jane Cook (William and Mary's eldest daughter) ran the company until 1934. (*Above: Gretchen Danckwardt. Below: Sue Turner*)

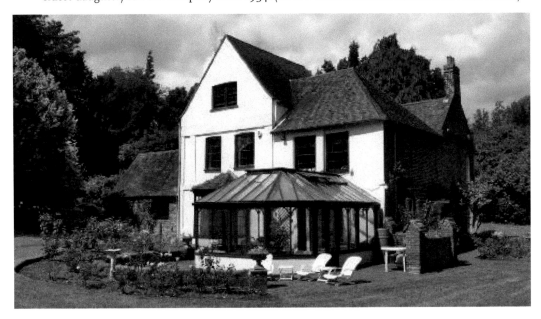

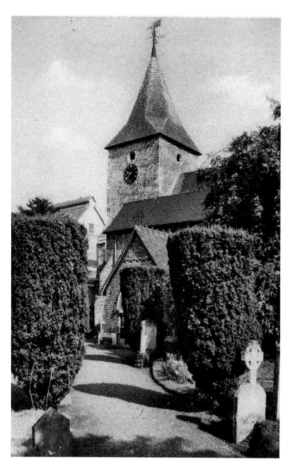

St Mary the Virgin, c. 1950
This is St Mary the Virgin parish church to St Mary Cray, dating back to the mid-thirteenth century. Now in a quiet cul-de-sac created by redirecting through traffic, the church would have been flanked to the east by the busy, bustling St Mary Cray High Street and the west by the multi-mill powering River Cray. The church continues to serve the local community in the way it has done for the past 750 years. The whole area around this part of the High Street is quite rightly a conservation area. (*Left: Lynn Sculpher Collection*)

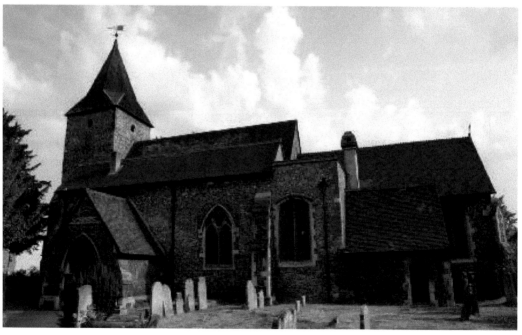

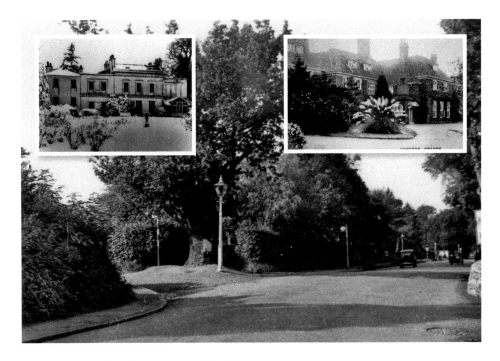

The Crofton Oak at the Junction of Crofton Road/Avenue, c. 1954
The Crofton oak at the junction of Crofton Road/Avenue (*c.* 1954), Crofton Grange (*c.* 1909) and Crofton Hall (*c.* 1930). An iconic natural landmark for centuries, the oak stood on the corner of Crofton Lane and Crofton Avenue, within sight of Crofton Grange, and five minutes' walk from Crofton Hall. A furniture delivery van hit the tree in 1967, causing irreparable damage, and many centuries of existence were cut down within hours. The grange and the hall had been purchased by the property developers of the day, and by the late 1950s both had disappeared. (*Above: Bromley Local Studies Department*)

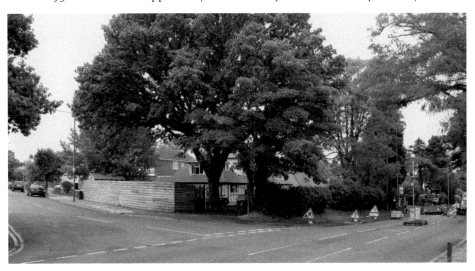

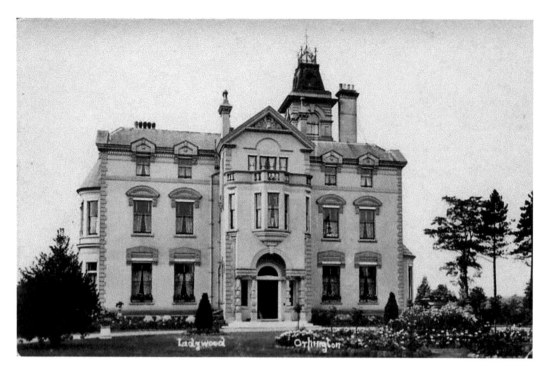

Ladywood, c. 1910
This beauty, Ladywood House, was originally built in 1874 in an estate of 120 acres, and was a prestigious dwelling occupied by lords and gentry until the Great Depression. In 1925, it met the same fate as Town Court Farm and parts of Poverest Farm, when it was sold by Basil Scruby as plots to develop the Petts Wood area. Princes Avenue and the Chenies now occupy the space where it stood.

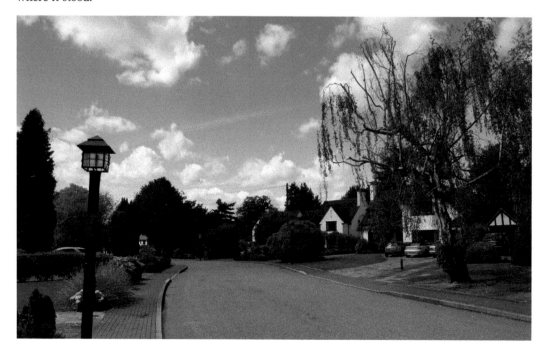

Crofton Place, 1964

Crofton Place is one of Orpington Urban District Council's last large residential developments. Built in the 1960s on the former Place Farm and Broom Wood, the estate boasted seven different types of dwelling, including fashionable town houses. Oil-fired central heating systems were installed in the vast majority of houses, with fuel available from huge underground tanks around the estate, installed by BP. A number of covenants on the land ensure the upkeep of public areas and footpaths, which sometimes follow old bridleways.

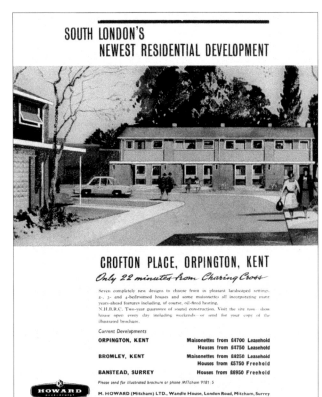

SOUTH LONDON'S
NEWEST RESIDENTIAL DEVELOPMENT

CROFTON PLACE, ORPINGTON, KENT

Only 22 minutes from Charing Cross

Seven completely new designs to choose from in pleasant landscaped settings. 2-, 3- and 4-bedroomed houses and some maisonettes all incorporating many years-ahead features including, of course, oil-fired heating.
N.H.B.R.C. Two-year guarantee of sound construction. Visit the site now – show house open every day including weekends – or send for your copy of the illustrated brochure.

Current Developments

ORPINGTON, KENT	Maisonettes from £4700	Leasehold
	Houses from £4750	Leasehold
BROMLEY, KENT	Maisonettes from £4250	Leasehold
	Houses from £5750	Freehold
BANSTEAD, SURREY	Houses from £6950	Freehold

Please send for illustrated brochure or phone MITcham 9181 5

HOWARD DEVELOPMENT

M. HOWARD (Mitcham) LTD., Wandle House, London Road, Mitcham, Surrey

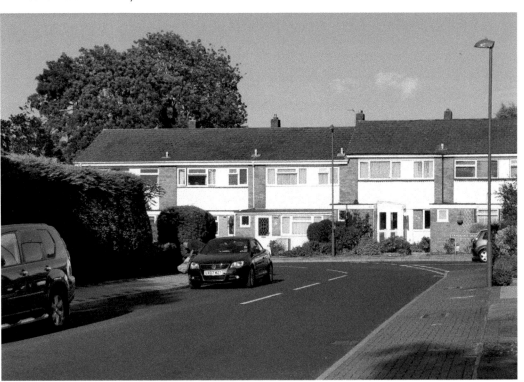

51

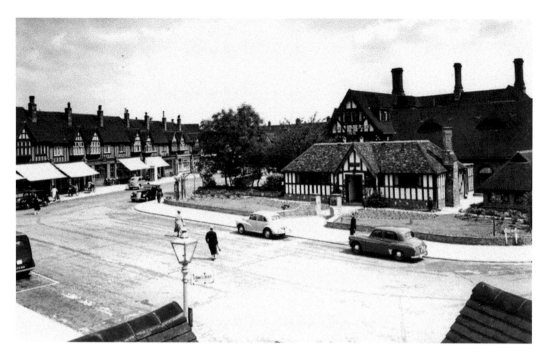

Petts Wood Station Square, 1954 and *c.* 1970

The station has been at the heart of Petts Wood 'village' since the railway split the area in two. Both the east and west sides had comprised farmland and estates with large houses, later developed into a suburban area, and currently dominated by 1920s and 1930s mock-Tudor architecture. Prior to suburban development, the woods belonging to the Pett family were leased for shipbuilding; the *Sovereign of the Seas* was built with Petts Wood timber in the late sixteenth century. (*Above: Lynn Sculpher Collection*)

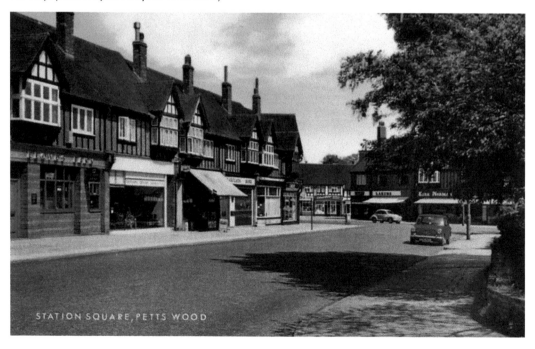

STATION SQUARE, PETTS WOOD

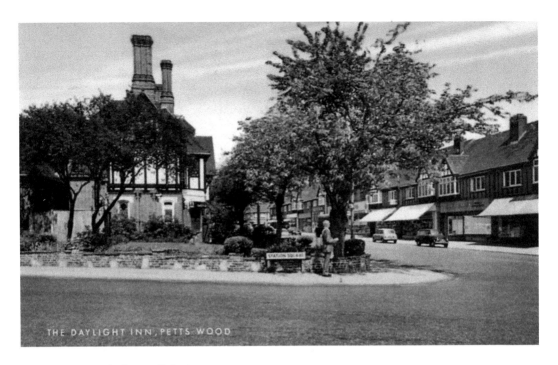

Petts Wood, the Daylight Inn, *c.* 1970

The inn was constructed and opened in 1935. Its current signage represents Daylight Saving Time (DST). Although DST was 'invented' by New Zealander George Vernon Hudson, it came into widespread use as a result of the work of Chislehurst resident William Willett. Following his 'eureka moment' in Petts Wood, the idea gained momentum during the First World War, and subsequently the majority of countries now put their clocks forward one hour in the summer. There is a stone memorial to Willett in Petts Wood. (*Above: Lynn Sculpher Collection*)

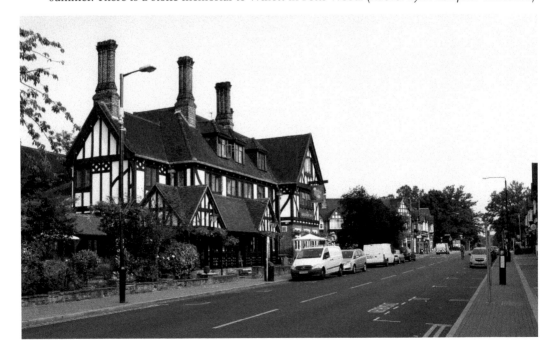

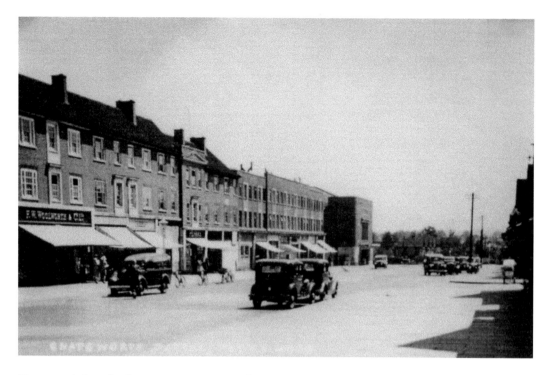

Chatsworth Parade, Queensway, Petts Wood, *c.* 1950
Purpose-built and relatively new in the older image, Queensway is, for all intents and purposes, Petts Wood High Street. You can see the former Woolworths to the left, and the Embassy Cinema can be seen further along to the left, just where Morrisons supermarket stands today.

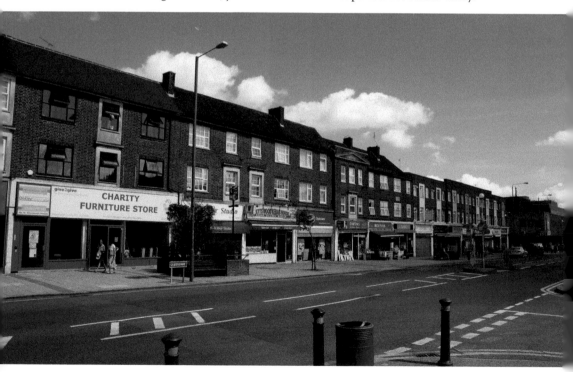

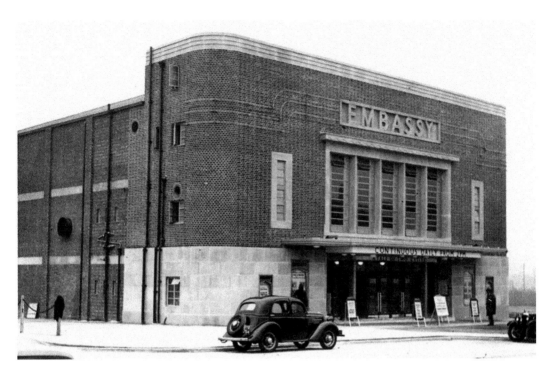

The Embassy Cinema, Queensway, Petts Wood, *c.* 1936

This beauty is the Embassy Cinema. 1,360 people could fit in here! After it closed in 1973, it remained derelict for a long time. The Morrisons supermarket (formerly Safeway) was built on its site and opened in 1982.

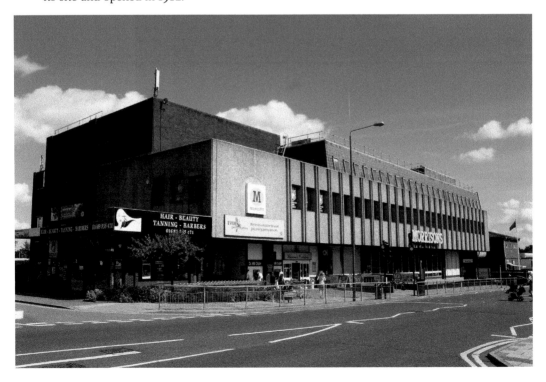

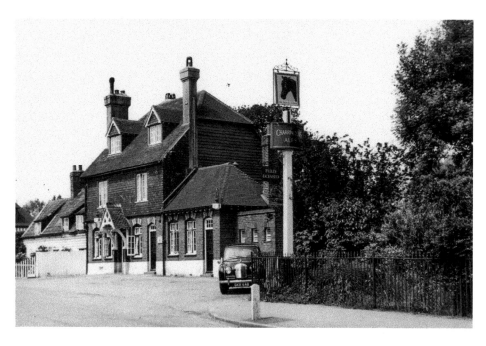

The Black Horse, Crofton Road, Locksbottom, *c.* 1955
As part of Farnborough, Locksbottom gained its patronage from three main sources: Godendene Farm (now the site of Sainsbury's and its immense car park), the workhouse, later the hospital (now the site of the Princess Royal University Hospital) and the trade from passers-by, coming through the junction of the main roads. The Black Horse is almost opposite Tugmutton Common, which is passionately preserved today by the Crofton Residents' Association as part of the former Ancient Hamlet and Manor of Crofton. (*Above: Bromley Local Studies Department*)

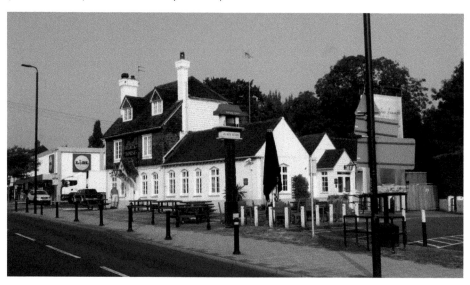

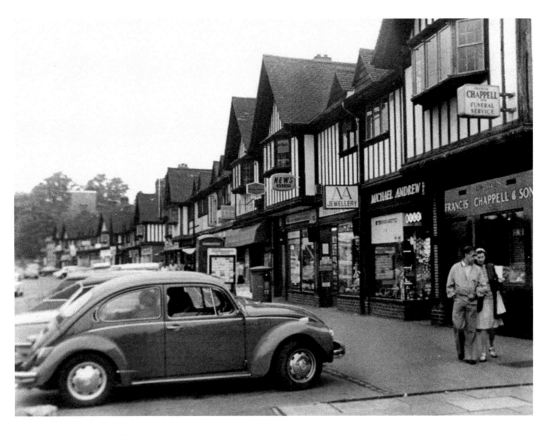

Locksbottom Shops, 1978

The Bromley Poor Law Union built a workhouse at Locksbottom in 1844. Over the years, more buildings were added, including an infirmary and a chapel – currently the sole original building that remains on the former workhouse site. The infirmary evolved into Farnborough Hospital in the early twentieth century and housed the district's main maternity centre. As a result, many residents of the area have 'Farnborough Kent' as their birthplace. The Princess Royal University Hospital has now replaced Farnborough Hospital.

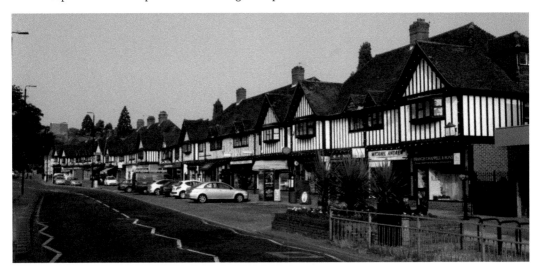

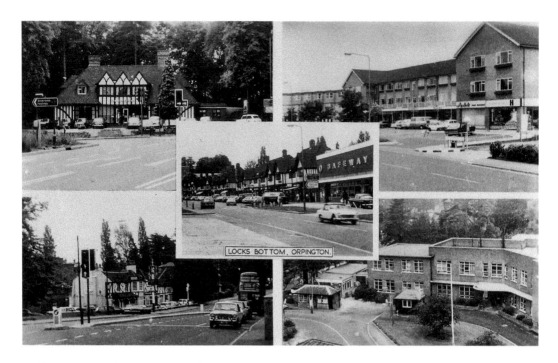

Locksbottom, Multi-View Postcard, *c.* 1980

This creative multi-picture postcard shows what the postcard creator thought were Locksbottom's interesting scenes. The shopping parade has existed since the 1920s and served the local residents of Farnborough and Keston Park. Most do not know that these affluent and highly sought-after premium addresses are nearly 100 years old! The Fantail Restaurant (now Chapter One) has always been a premium restaurant location. Another scene shows the entrance to the former Farnborough Hospital.

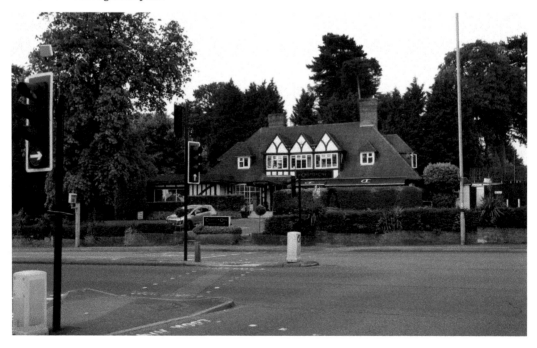

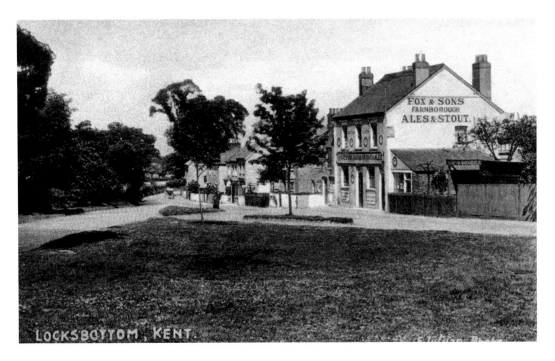

The British Queen, Locksbottom, *c.* 1890

This view of Crofton Road from around 1890 speaks volumes. The British Queen public house (at the time of print sadly closed) shows off the advertising of its brewer, Fox & Sons of Green Street Green. At this time, Locksbottom was part of Farnborough. The main road from London to the Cinque Ports of Rye and Hastings passes across the north of the village. The road from Orpington, via Crofton, comes up from the south and the road from Croydon, via the Keston Mark, comes in from the north. (*Above: Peter Reeve*)

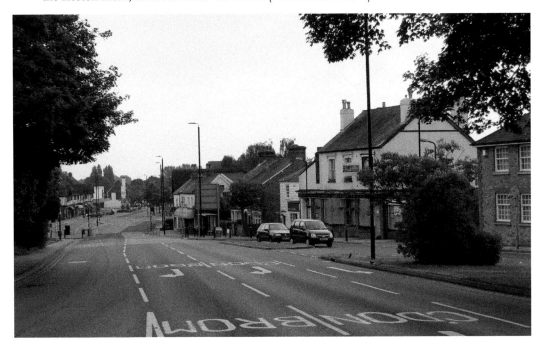

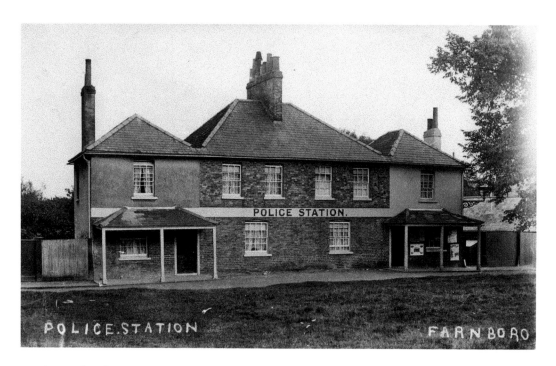

Farnborough Police Station, *c.* 1908

Built in 1839, Farnborough police station was one of the first stations to be sited strategically along a key trading route; the London Road from Bromley Common was infamous for hijacks and highway robbery. Together with St Mary Cray police station, the Farnborough police station served most of the Orpington District for well over 100 years, until the new police station at Orpington was opened in 1984. Thankfully, the old buildings remain in place, and are virtually unchanged. (*Above: Peter Reeve*)

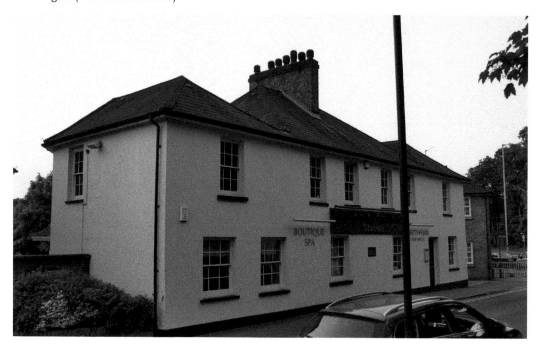

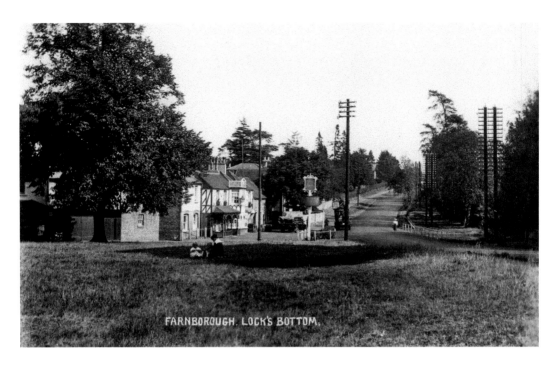

Ye Olde Whyte Lyon, *c.* 1910

A view of the main road to Hastings and Rye showing Ye Olde Whyte Lyon coaching inn. The White Lion (in today's tongue) was built in 1626, and provided stabling and a place for travellers to rest, in a fairly isolated location, on the coastal route from London. The building would have heard tales from travelling traders during the Civil War, and talk of highwaymen and tales of hijacks. The current building retains immense character and is another jewel in the crown of our district's heritage. (*Above: Peter Reeve*)

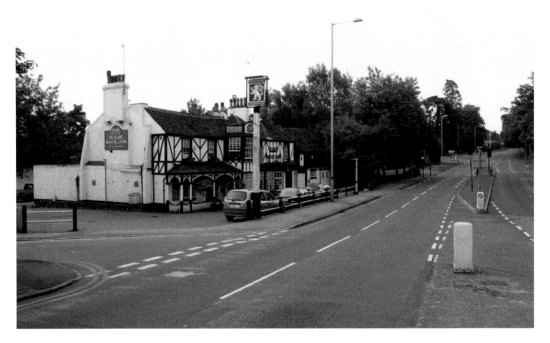

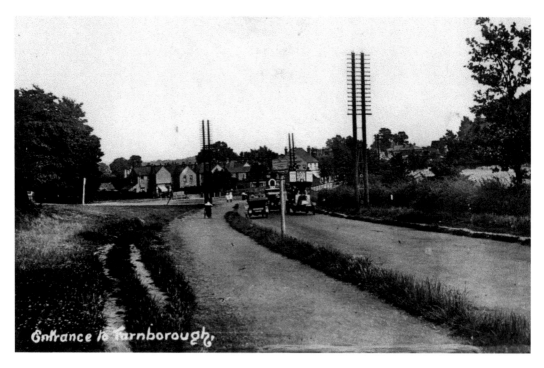

Farnborough Common, Looking East, c. 1915
This is the view of the main coast road looking east towards Farnborough before the bypass would take the road around the village. The bypass would disconnect the Board School from the village and also slice through the small common.

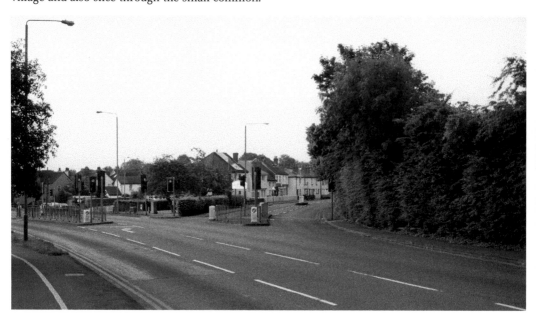

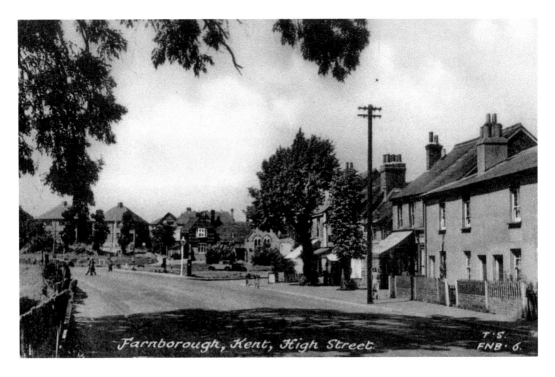

Farnborough High Street, Looking West Towards the Board School, *c.* 1930
This view has not changed much at all. Before the bypass was built, there was a common in front of the Board School. Today it is a small piece of land marooned between the road junction of Starts Hill, Farnborough High Street and the A21.

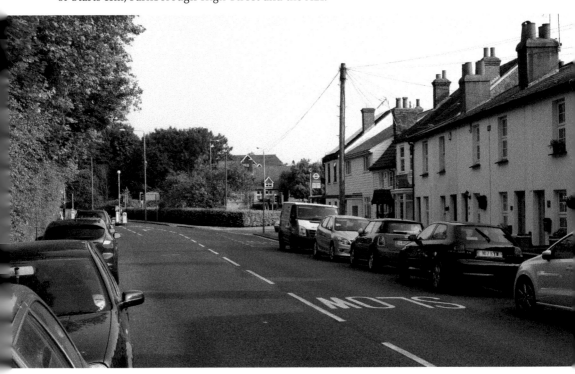

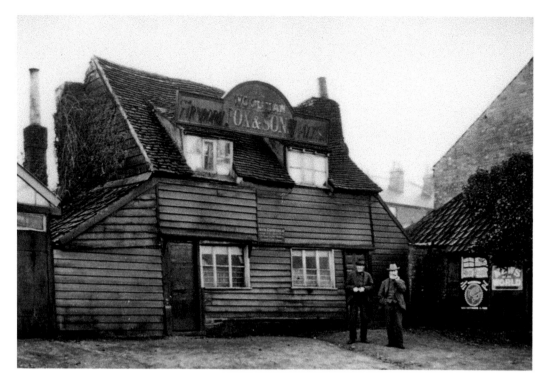

The Woodman Public House, c. 1890

The Woodman has existed successfully for centuries alongside its village public house contemporaries. The Woodman didn't have the coaching stage of the George and was, perhaps, less salubrious than the New Inn (Change of Horses), but it has always been a regular and popular venue within the village. In the old image you will see the original 'wooden' Woodman! The brewery advertised was the local Fox's Brewery of Green Street Green. Today, the Woodman continues to offer great hospitality, varied cask ales, food and regular entertainment activities! (*Above: Peter Reeve*)

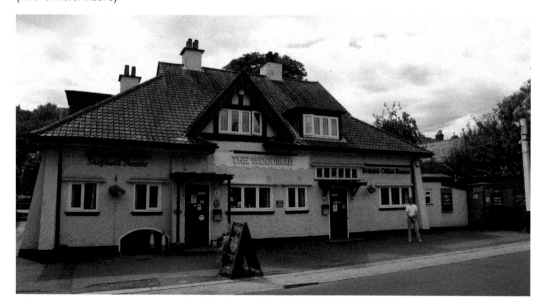

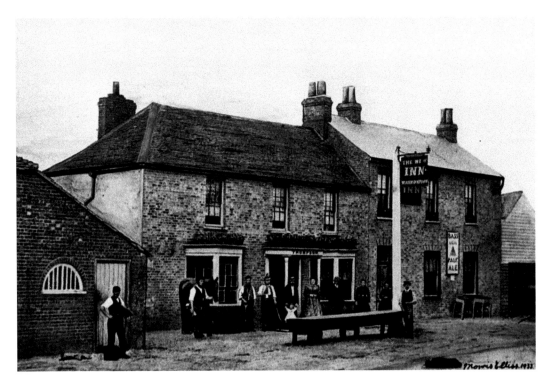

Farnborough High Street, the New Inn, c. 1933
A pub has existed on this site for over 200 years in one form or another. The New Inn was New for a very long time and then renamed the Change of Horses. As mentioned, the public houses of Farnborough not only served the local people but also provided rest and refreshment for travelling folk.

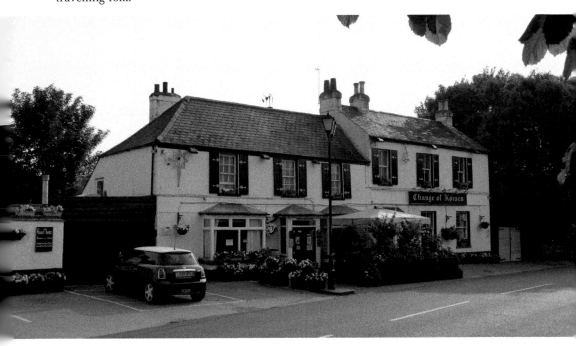

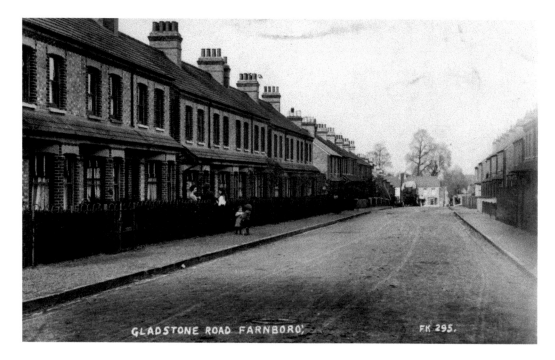

Farnborough, Gladstone Road, c. 1910

Named after William Gladstone, popular Liberal Prime Minister. In the 1850s, the West End of London and Crystal Palace Railway (WELCPR) planned to extend their railway from Crystal Palace to Farnborough. By 1858, the line ran from Crystal Palace to Beckenham Junction and then extended to Shortlands (called Bromley) and stopped. Likewise, the East Kent Railway (later the London Chatham and Dover Railway) built their line from Strood (via St Mary Cray) to Shortlands. A Farnborough railway never materialised. However, Farnborough village's inheritance was a fine collection of typical late period Victorian terraced houses – built for the workers and potential residents the railway never brought!

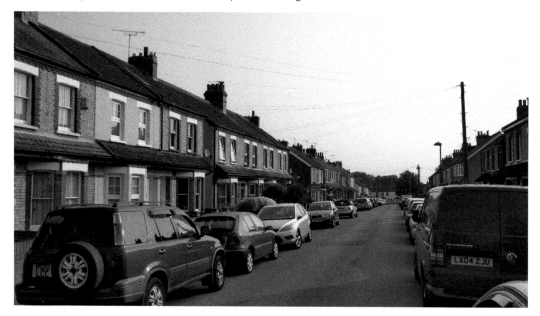

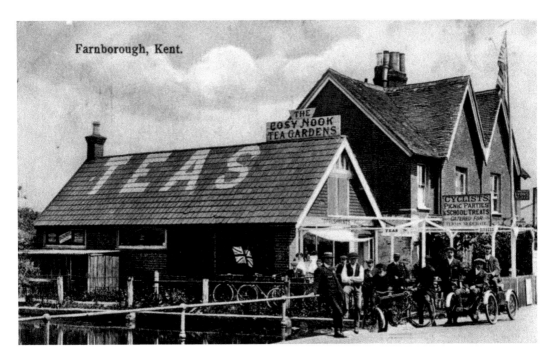

Farnborough, Kent.

Farnborough, High Street, the Cosy Nook, c. 1920

For hundreds of years, Farnborough was an important stop-off point to change or rest horses and refresh travellers on the main coaching route from London to the Cinque Ports of Rye and Hastings. By the early twentieth century, with the arrival of the Omnibus routes to/from London and more free time, Farnborough became a popular leisure destination for ramblers, cyclists and locals alike. The Cosy Nook was one of many tea rooms that traded successfully alongside the traditional public houses in those carefree days!

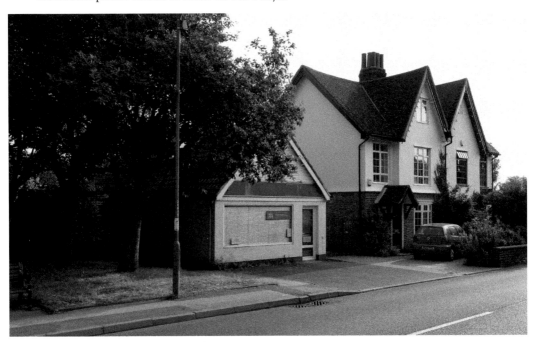

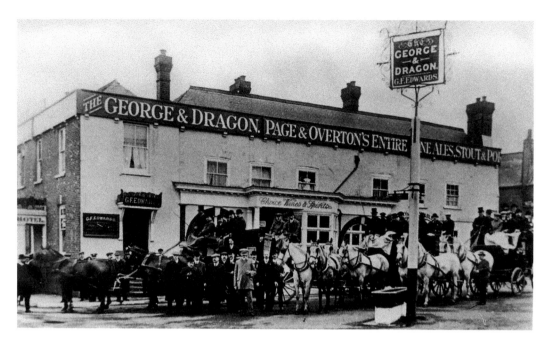

Farnborough, George & Dragon, *c. 1910 (above), c. 1920 (below)*

The original George & Dragon (later the George) dated back to the sixteenth century, and was a significant inn for a village the size of Farnborough. It stood on the corner of Farnborough High Street and Church Road where Church Hill was the route onward to Pratts Bottom, via Old Hill, not Farnborough Hill as some believed. The George became a terminus for one of the first regular bus routes, helping the village establish itself as a leisure venue.

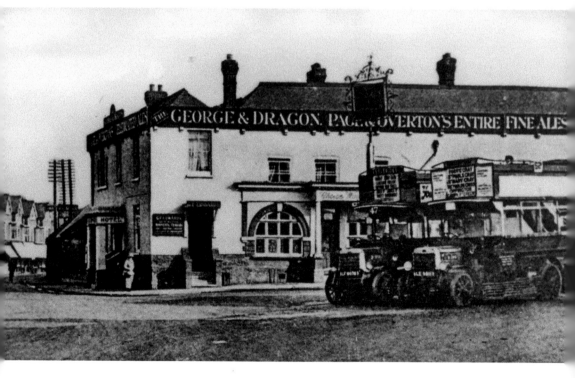

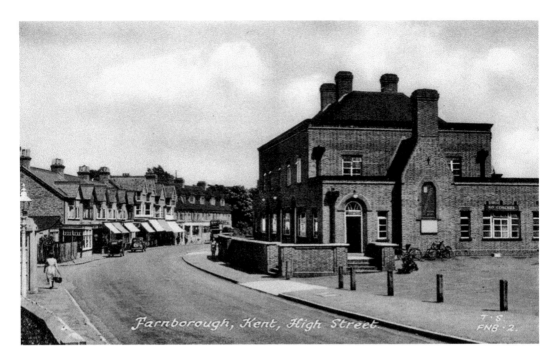

Farnborough, High Street, the George, *c.* 1930

The George of the 1920s and 1930s specifically catered for the hundreds of ramblers and cyclists who would descend on the area – usually on a Sunday afternoon. The growing motor traffic also stopped en route to the coast. In the 1930s, a new building replaced the sixteenth-century one. Sadly, in 2003, the demise of through traffic and a change in social behaviour resulted in the George closing. The former buildings were knocked down and residential dwellings built.

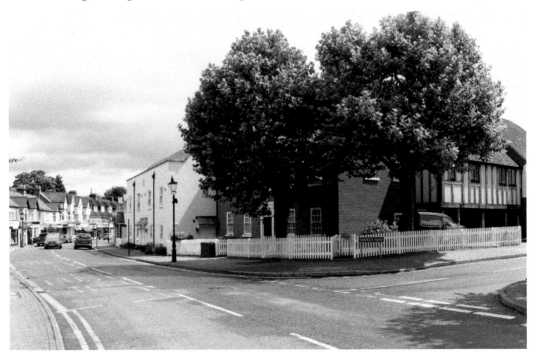

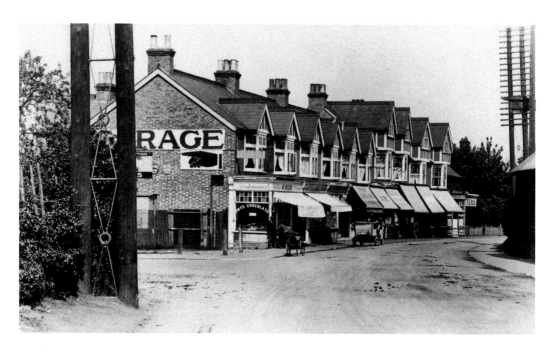

Farnborough, High Street, Main Parade, c. 1920

Farnborough Hill was constructed to provide a better route to the north of Green Street Green High Street and to recover the route south to Pratts Bottom. This resulted in traffic no longer travelling down Church Hill. Between 1871 and 1921, Farnborough's residential population grew from over 1,000 to almost 4,400! Shops became a priority to support this growth. The main parade of new shops associated with Farnborough High Street can be seen in their Edwardian splendour in the old image above. Shops in the village continue to prosper, offering locals something traditional, convenient and within walking distance.

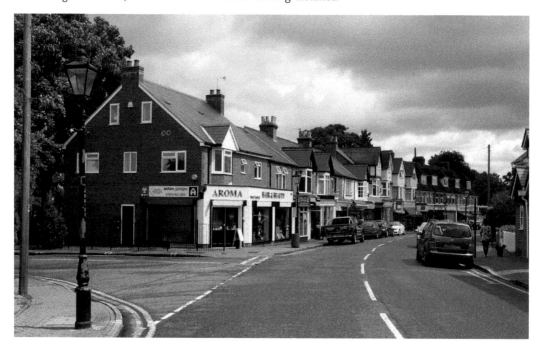

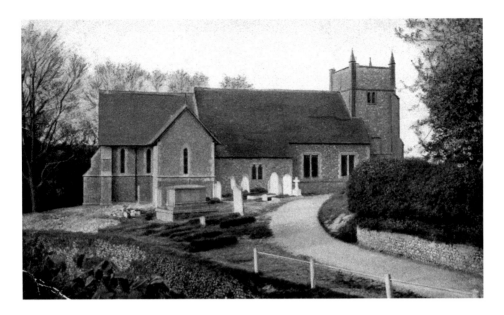

Farnborough, St Giles Church, *c.* 1907

'Fearn Biorg' (meaning ferns on the hill) references go back to Anglo–Saxon AD 862 and for at least 1,500 years there has been a chapel or church on this site. Although the Norman Domesday Book does not record the existence of a chapel at Farnborough, it is almost certain that one did. In the early Norman period of the eleventh century, Bishop Gandulf was both Lord of the Manor of Chelsfield and Farnborough. Gandulf would have based himself at the larger estate at Chelsfield and had a church and priest there. The Chelsfield priest also attended 'Faernberga' chapel. Chelsfield and Farnborough would not have their own rectors until 1650. Parts of the church at Farnbrough are thought to originate from the twelfth century. The churchyard is of great importance, as the resting place of may prominent locals.

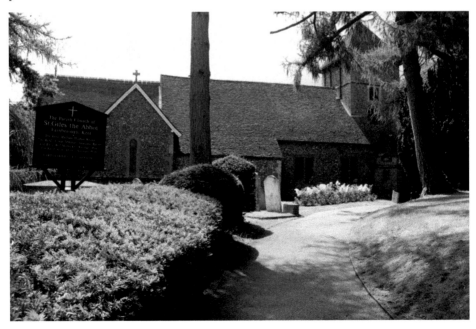

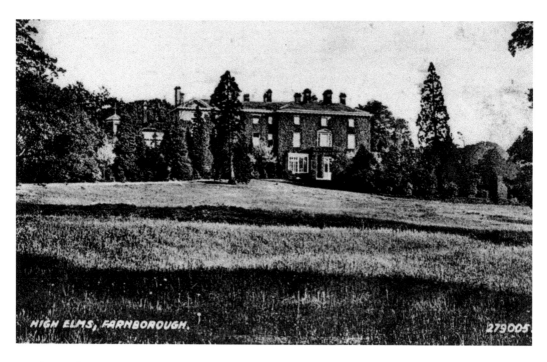

Farnborough, High Elms House, *c.* 1915

From the early nineteenth century, High Elms House and Estate belonged to the Lubbock family. In 1865, ownership passed to Sir John William Lubbock (4th Baronet and 1st Lord Avebury). His prestigious philanthropic, scientific and political careers and friendship with Darwin made him and High Elms famous. We have him to thank for the Bank Holiday Act 1871! The Lubbocks sold the house in 1938, which burned to the ground in 1967. Today the estate is a popular recreation and education centre.

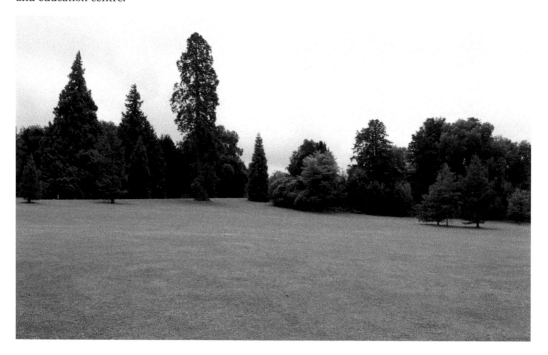

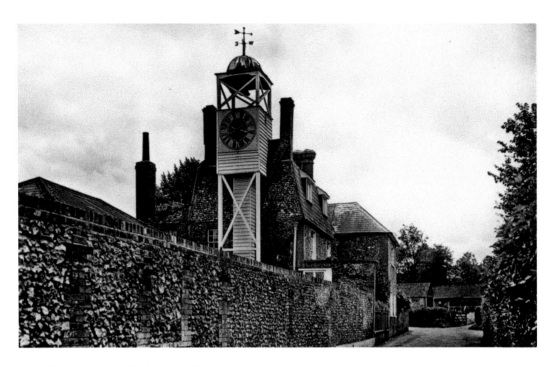

Farnborough, Clock House Farm, *c.* 1940

This is one of the original nineteenth-century buildings of the original High Elms Estate, and here is the farmhouse of what is now called Clock House Farm. In 1826, the clock and bell were constructed to give a visible and audible call to the workers to mark the start and end of the working day and meal times.

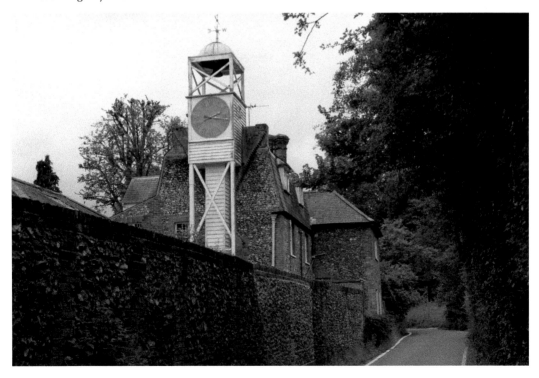

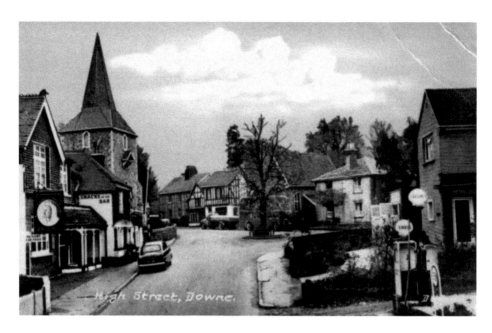

Downe High Street, *c.* 1950

This view from around 1950 has remained virtually unchanged for over 100 years. The renowned Charles Darwin moved to Downe House in 1842 and worked there on his theories of evolution by natural selection. Darwin was great friends with Sir John Lubbock and they shared their work on natural studies. Although Darwin's Downe House is a popular tourist attraction, Downe remains a pretty, picturesque village with an old oak tree, pubs and village shops.

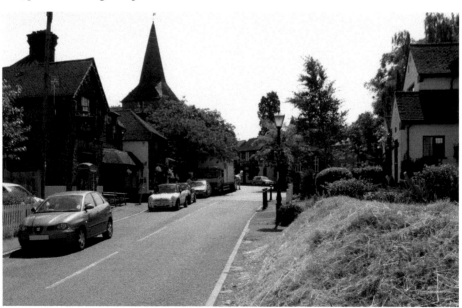

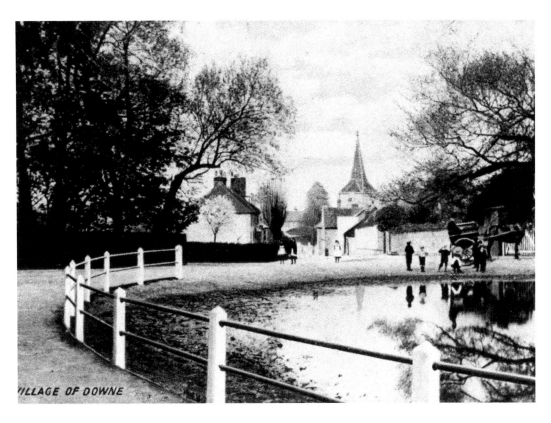

VILLAGE OF DOWNE

Downe Village, *c.* 1890
A view across the pond. Again, a picturesque view, which has not changed in centuries, although some of you looking at these images who know Downe may have noticed something has dried up! (*Above: Philip Lane Collection*)

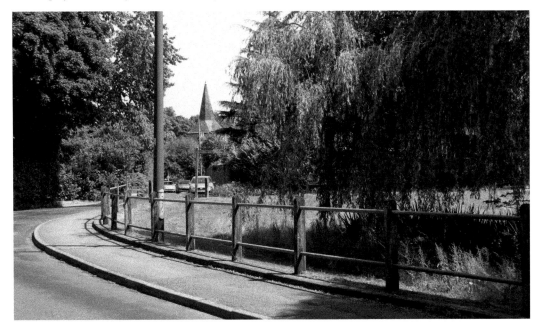

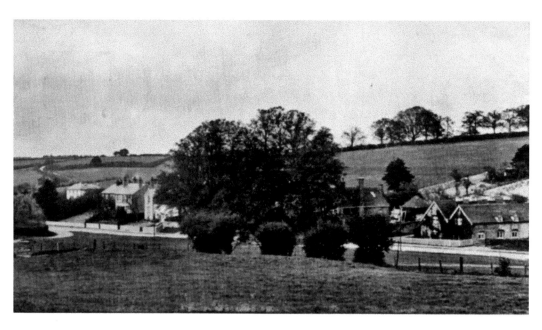

Pratts Bottom Green, *c.* 1908

Pratts Bottom, so named after the Pratt family who were early landowners here, was a hamlet in the parish of Chelsfield. The main road to the coast originally passed through here, with a toll-gate established after the road was turnpiked in 1747. The Bull's Head was an important coaching inn until the new road via Polhill, avoiding Rushmore Hill and, still more, the steep slope of Star Hill, was opened in the 1830s, after which the prosperity of the hamlet declined.

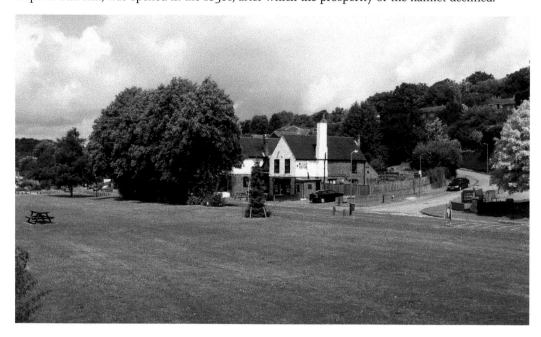

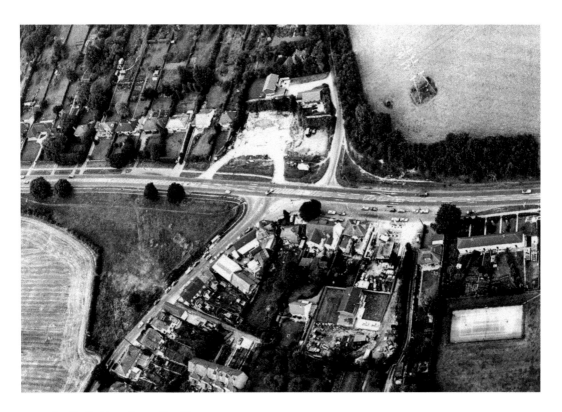

Pratts Bottom from the Air, 1975

This photograph shows Pratts Bottom has developed in more recent times. The fortunes of the hamlet began to revive after the building of Chelsfield and Knockholt stations, with many railway workers living here in newly built cottages. A further impetus was given by the opening of George Osgood's Carriage Works in 1889, while more recently the hamlet has become popular among London commuters. Despite new developments, Pratts Bottom, set in beautiful surrounding open country, has retained its village character. (*Above: Philip Lane Collection*)

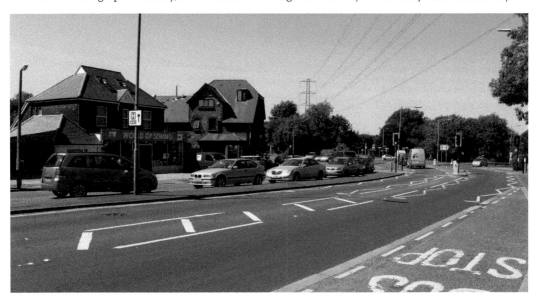

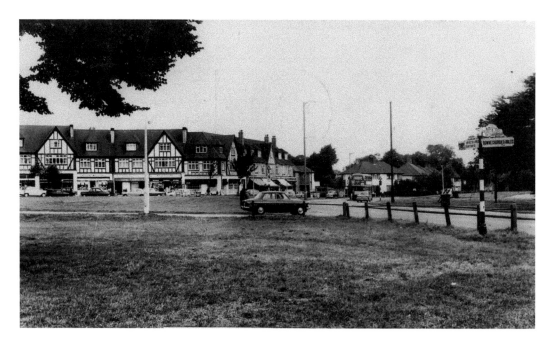

Crescent Way, Sevenoaks Road, *c.* 1970
This crescent-shaped double parade of shops was built as part of the Davis Estate that surrounds the immediate area. The residential development was started in the 1930s and completed after the Second World War. During the war, numbers of half-built properties and roads were simply left until they could be completed. This is why the estate has two distinct styles of housing, from the 1930s and the 1950s.

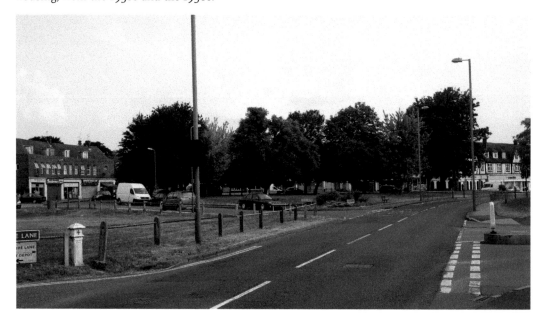

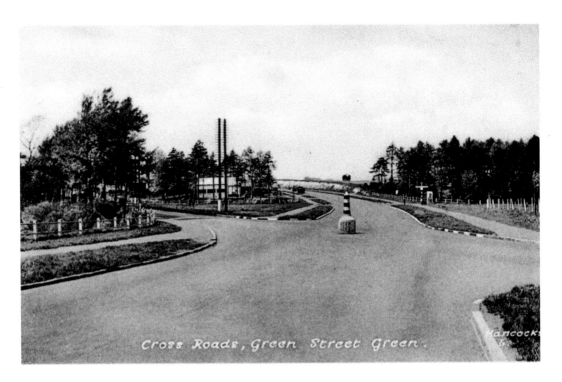

Farnborough Bypass Crossroads, c. 1935

This junction was created as a result of the construction of the bypass. Originally, Shire Lane continued to Sevenoaks Road and to a junction with Warren Road. Farnborough Hill continued into the part of Farnborough Hill that leads into Green Street Green. The junction would be attended by an AA Officer directing traffic by hand signals. Imagine how effective this junction marker would have been in the dark or bad weather! (*Above: David Daws*)

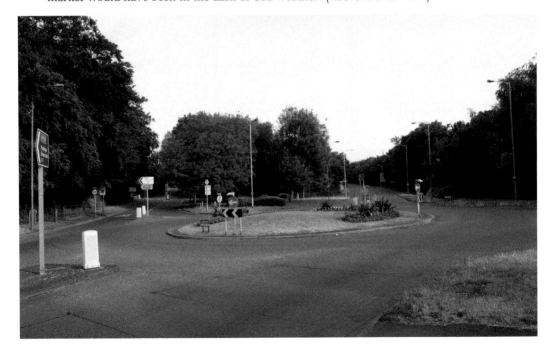

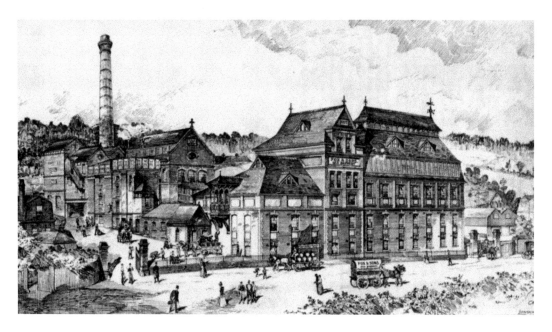

Green Street Green, Fox & Son Oak Brewery, *c.* 1850 and *c.* 1915

In 1818, John Fox moved to Green Street Green to run Oak Farm and, as was common, grew his own hops and grain to produce ale for family use, selling the excess to the Lubbock family. Encouraged by Sir John Lubbock, John Fox started brewing commercially and by 1836, Oak Brewery produced ale. Business boomed, the brewery expanded, and local pubs proudly displayed the Fox name. The Fox family contributed hugely to the development of Green Street Green and the welfare of its residents, many of whom were employees. Foxes ceased trading in 1909 and the huge brewery was ultimately demolished. The last factory on the site used the brewery perimeter wall as its own, as well as the huge cellars and chambers underground. All buildings were finally demolished and filled in. A pleasant housing estate now exists on the land. (*Above: Bromley Local Studies Department*)

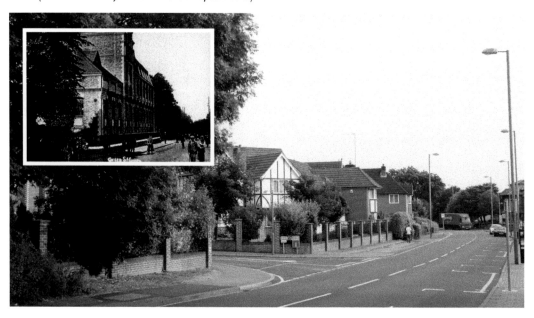

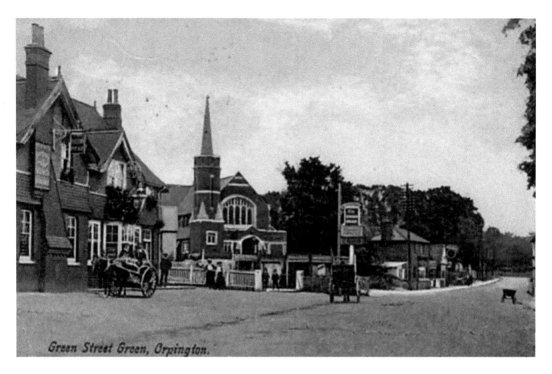

Green Street Green, Orpington.

Green Street Green, Queens Head and Baptist Church, *c.* 1910

The Queens Head, one of three public houses in Green Street Green, is still a popular venue for the village. The Baptist church was built following sufficient expansion in the congregation to make it viable. Early in the nineteenth century, Green Street Green was a small hamlet. It became a village in its own right following expansion resulting from the success of the Oak Brewery and redirection of the coast road down Farnborough Hill and into the main street.

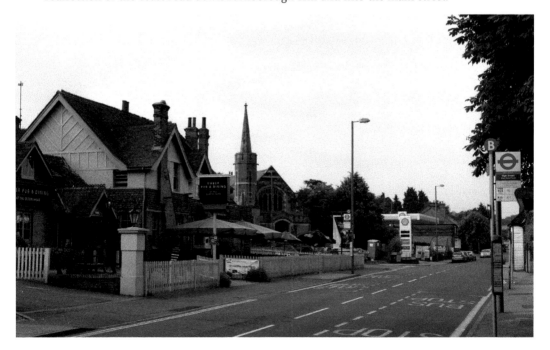

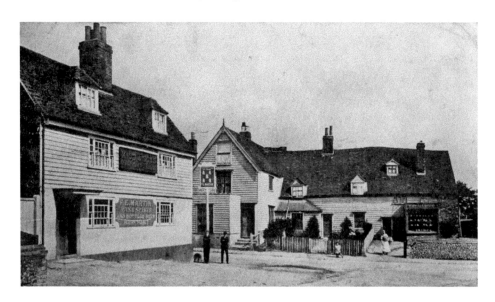

The Five Bells Public House, Chelsfield

We are so lucky that, as shown in this view of Chelsfield village's pub, *c.* 1907, many of the typical scenes of villages within the district have not changed all that much. Chelsfield ecclesiastical parish was originally of considerable extent, including the hamlet of Pratts Bottom and part of Green Street Green. The building of the Orpington Bypass (Court Road) in the 1920s unfortunately cut off the church and the court lodge from the village. (*Above: Jean Bodfish Collection*)

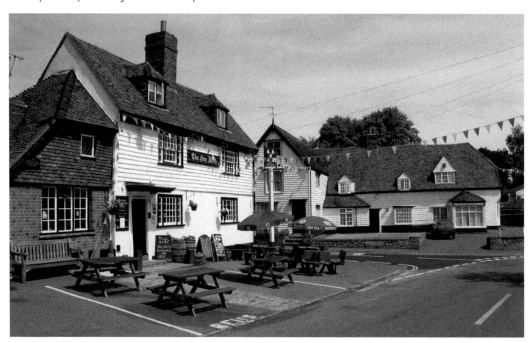

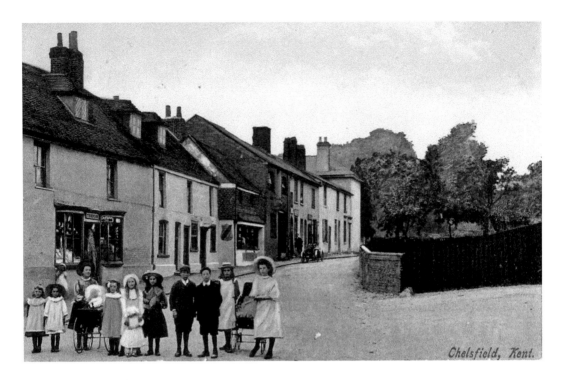

Chelsfield High Street, *c.* 1908
This is a well-known image of a line-up of local children taken in about 1908, in an unusual coloured version. This style of colouring cost the shopkeeper a little more but gave him an edge over competitors. In those days, postcard messages were the equivalent of email today; when Royal Mail had many collections and deliveries, postcards often took just a few hours to be delivered. (*Above: Jean Bodfish Collection*)

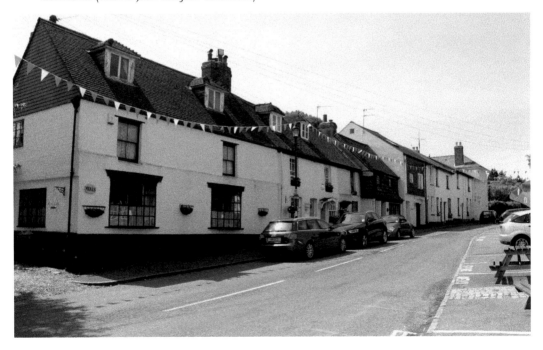

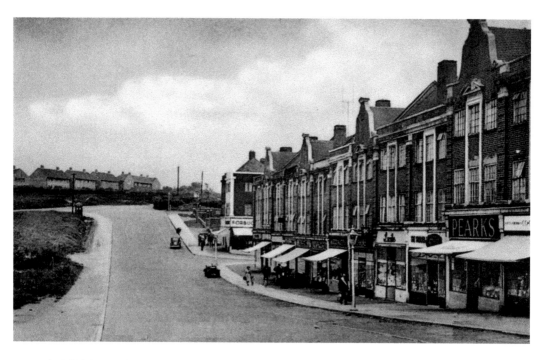

New Chelsfield, Windsor Drive, *c.* 1950
Chelsfield railway station was opened in 1868 in an area then entirely surrounded by open land. The coming of the railway lead to some new housing at Pratts Bottom, where many railway workers lived, and at Green Street Green, where Fox's Brewery had many employees. However, the area closer to the station remained largely farmland until the building of the Chelsfield Park Estate, which began in 1920, while 'New Chelsfield', including Windsor Drive, was developed from 1933 onwards.

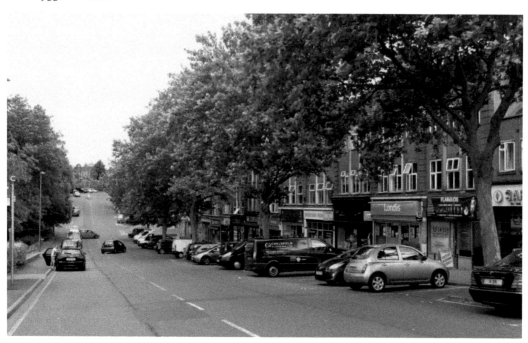

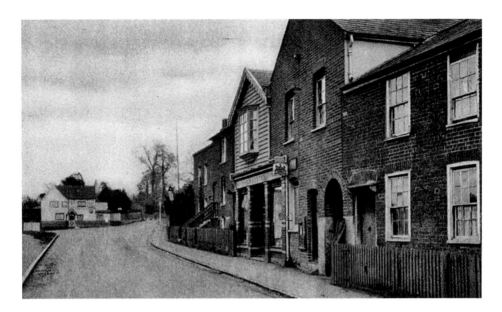

Main Road, St Paul's Cray, *c.* 1900

Around 1900, St Paul's Cray comprised of St Paulinus church, the Bull pub, a small number of dispersed houses, Coppice Wood, Gray's Farm, St Paul's Cray Hill, St Paul's Cray Common and a corn mill powered by the River Cray. The older image shows St Paulinus and the junction where the Bull pub is located – these were then the origin and focal points of the parish. It was an important point for travellers bound for Foots Cray, Sidcup, Bexley and Maidstone. The corn mill became Nash's Paper Mill. Coppice Wood, St Paul's Cray Hill and Gray's Farm would become housing estates following the Second World War housing boom.

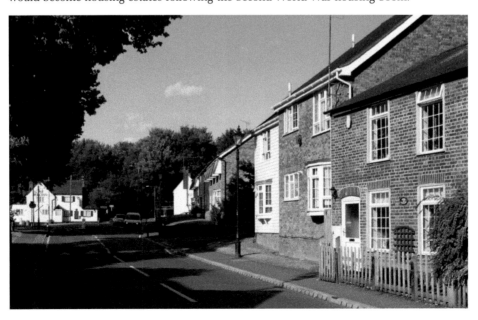

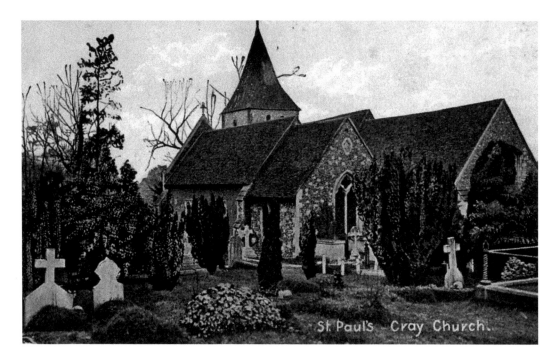

St Paulinus, *c.* 1900

This ancient parish church has registers going back to 1580. The origins of the church go further back to Saxon times. St Paul's Cray was once part of the lathe of Sutton-at-Hone, hundred of Ruxley and within the Union of Bromley. It was an important part of the village. Sadly, the use of the church declined and the parish was withdrawn. However, a new chapter has begun with the Redeemed Christian Church of God reopening the church for religious worship. (*Above: Lynn Sculpher Collection*)

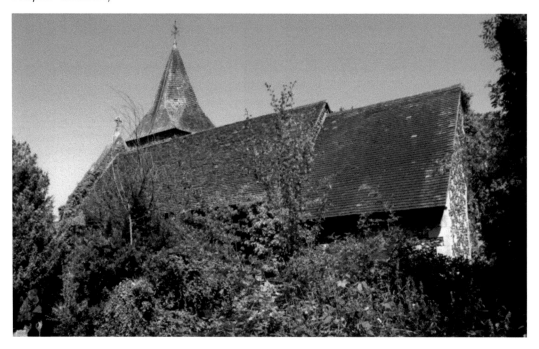

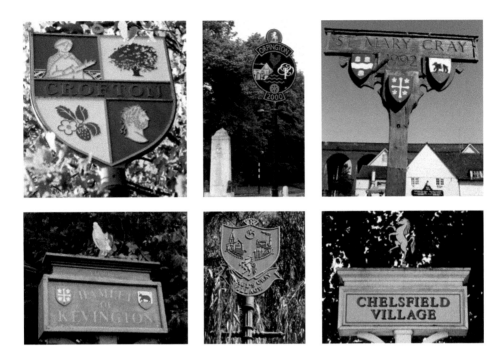

Crofton
Showing the former oak, an image of hop and strawberry pertaining to the large manor farms that operated in the area, and a Roman Emperor pertaining to Crofton Roman Villa.

Orpington
Showing the priory, the River Cray as the priory pond is the source, a walnut tree representing the former estate, house and name of local shopping centre, the Orpington chicken, the Kent Invicta. Erected in 2000 to celebrate the millennium.

St Mary Cray
Erected in 1992 to represent twenty-one years of the St Mary Cray Action Group. There are five family shields representing the most prominent of the former manors that made up the parish, plus the Kent Invicta.

Kevington
A former manor within St Mary Cray, the sign has two of the crests of the St Mary Cray sign representing the Onslow (the bear) and Manning families (red crest). Topped by the Orpington chicken.

St Paul's Cray
Showing the church of St Paulinus, an apple depicting the orchards of the area, the former Nash Paper Mill and the Kent Invicta.

Chelsfield
A simple named sign, with Kent Invicta, for this ancient parish.

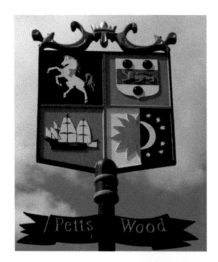
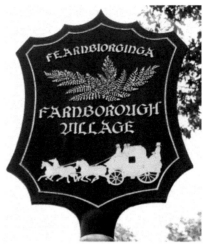

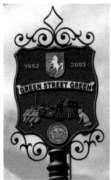
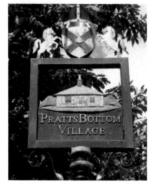
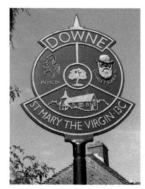

Petts Wood
Showing the Kent Invicta horse, the Pett family coat of arms, the *Sovereign of the Seas* (as built by Pett) and the daylight symbol relating to Mr William Willett, a local resident who proposed Daylight Saving.

Farnborough
Showing the ancient spelling for the village, which means Ferns on the Hill, depicted by an image of a fern, a horse-led coach, depicting a time when Farnborough was a popular and important coaching stop.

Green Street Green
Showing the former Fox's Oak Brewery, the Kent Invicta and a gold crown to represent the Golden Jubilee of HM Queen Elizabeth II.

Pratts Bottom
Showing the old toll-house at the bottom of Rushmore Hill, the heraldic arms of the Diocese of Rochester and the Kentish Invicta. Produced locally for the millennium celebrations.

Downe
Showing the thirteenth-century St Mary the Virgin parish church, its most famous former resident, Charles Darwin, and the old oak tree that is in the centre of the village.

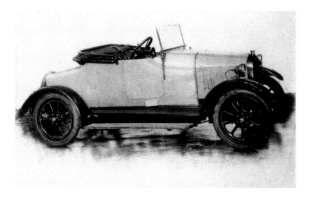 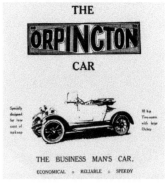

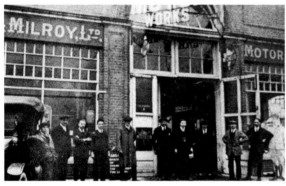 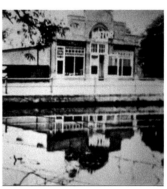

Smith and Milroy, *c.* 1920

The Orpington Car, built by Frank Smith and Jack Milroy at their works in Wellington Road (although the images here show their works at the northern end of Orpington High Street opposite the priory pond), was shown at the 1920 Motor Show. It was a two-seater convertible, with a dickey seat and a 10 horsepower 7kW engine. Although briefly successful, the last car was built in 1925. The only known survivor once appeared in the 1970s television series *Crossroads*. A recent publication, to which the Orpington History Organisation contributed images and information, is available. For further information please see www.theorpingtoncar.co.uk.

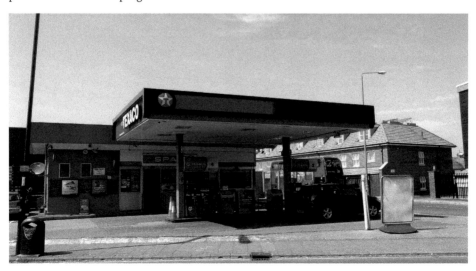

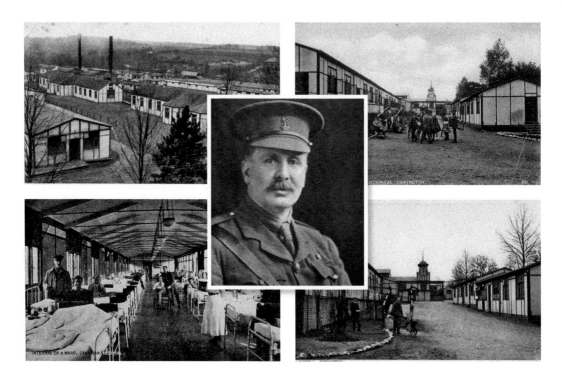

Orpington Hospital

The Ontario Military Hospital was built on the Boundary estate by the Ontario Canadian government in February 1916. The hospital served the Commonwealth soldiers of the First World War. By 1919, it was known as '16th Canadian General' and over 15,000 wounded soldiers were being treated here. The Canada Wing, Orpington Hospital, was opened in 1983, and is the only reminder left of a vast hospital that served the Commonwealth and became a civilian hospital serving the area for many years. Col D. W. McPherson, CO Ontario Hospital, is seen in the centre of the collage. The image below shows the current hospital (Canada Wing) and the 1916 clock, restored and placed in the modern hospital grounds.

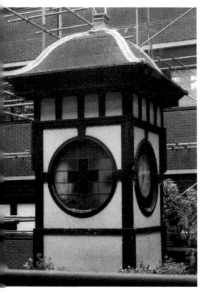
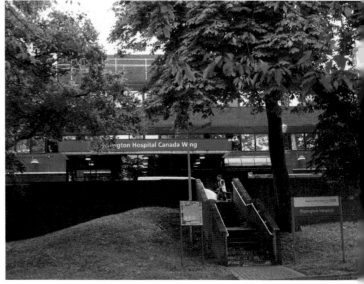

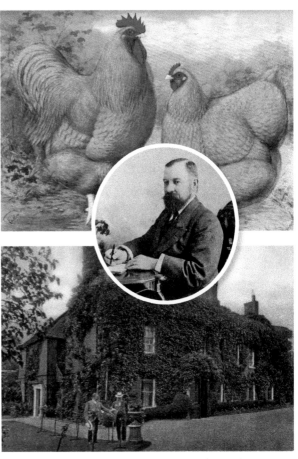

William Cook and William Henry Cook

As described earlier in the book, William Cook and his eldest son, William Henry, both ran poultry farms in the district based on the success of the Orpington chickens and ducks. The Buff Orpington is the most famous breed of Orpington chicken and is still actively bred around the world by farmers and individuals alike. William Cook was a prolific writer and created a number of well-publicised poultry-related publications.

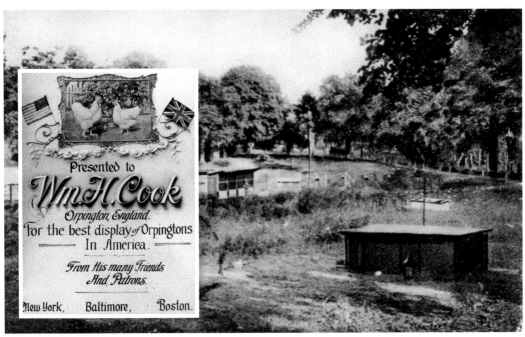

Presented to
Wm.H.Cook
Orpington, England.
For the best display of Orpingtons
In America.

From His many Friends
And Patrons.

New York.   Baltimore,   Boston.

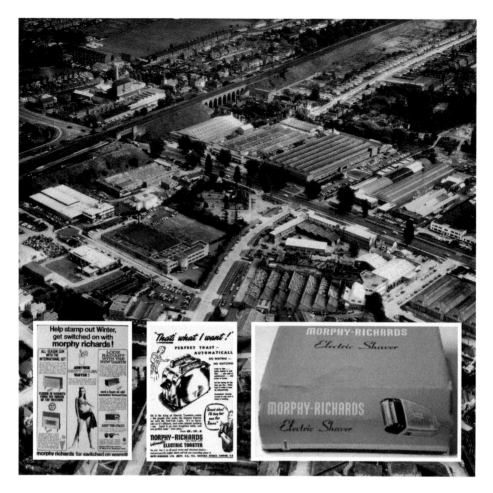

Morphy Richards of Manor Farm, St Mary Cray

Mr Donal Morphy and Mr Charles Richards had previously worked together, and on 8 July 1936 at Manor Farm, Market Meadow, St Mary Cray, 'Morphy Richards' started trading. The company, a household name nowadays and for decades before, established its headquarters and manufacturing premises at St Mary Cray. For nearly half a century, they were the biggest employer in the district. By 1970, production of goods moved to Swinton and Dundee.

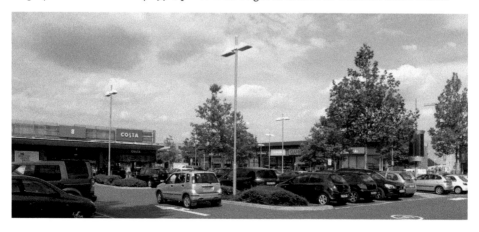

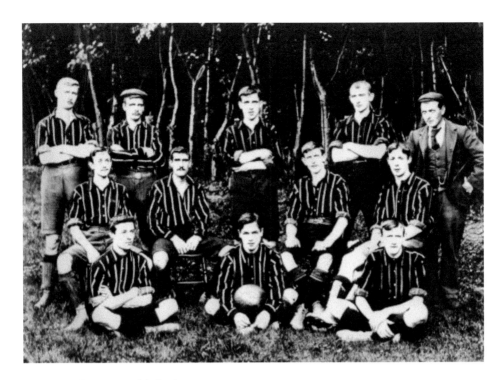

Cray Wanderers, Established 1860

Cray Wanderers was founded in 1860 and is reputed to be the oldest association football club in London and Kent and the joint second-oldest in the world. Over the years, Cray have won a succession of titles and cups, a list of which makes an impressive citation to their drive and determination, while the odds have often been stacked against them. Currently, the club is based at Hayes Lane, Bromley, where it has been ground-sharing with Bromley FC. Prior to this, Cray played their home games at Oxford Road in Sidcup, Grassmeade and Fordcroft in St Mary Cray. Stories and recollections of Cray Wanderers Football Club can now be read on the dedicated history website at www.craywands.co.uk. (*Trevor Mulligan*)

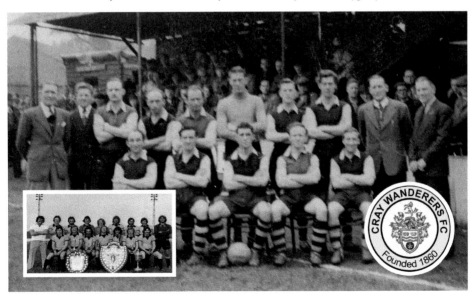

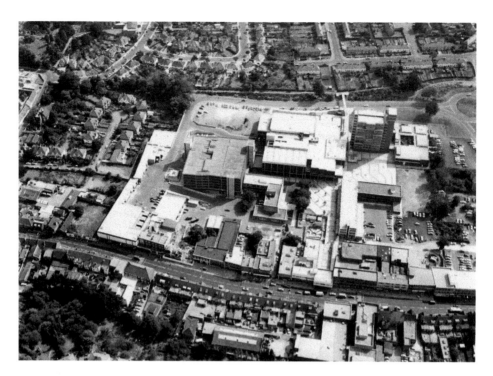

The Walnuts Shopping Centre, Leisure Centre and Orpington College, *c.* 1975
The High Street and the Walnuts Shopping Centre are going through challenging times of late. There is, however, positivity and commitment to bringing shoppers back, notwithstanding the multiplex cinema currently being constructed! In the older view, you can see the Walnuts Shopping Centre, leisure centre and Orpington College in what you could argue were the golden years. The area was previously made up of land owned by the council, the Walnuts House and grounds and parts of the former Court Lodge Farm. The college was built in 1972, the shopping centre opened in stages in 1973 and then fully by 1974, and the leisure centre was opened by the Queen Mother in 1975. (*Above: David Daws*)

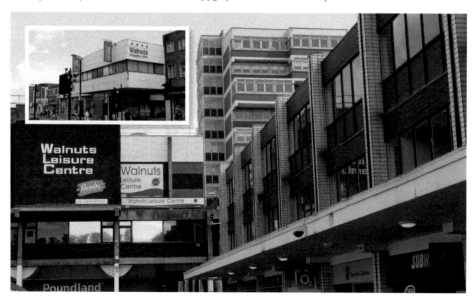

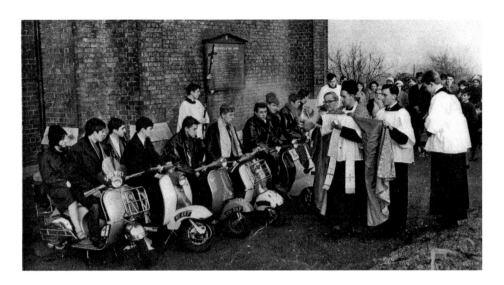

Facebook, Online Community Vote

At the time of the production of this book, a vote was cast on our hugely successful Facebook page. Seven of our most popular images (some already in this book on other pages) were shown and the community asked to vote. The clear winner were these images, which celebrated fifty years of the Orpington Scooter Mods. The images had originally been seen, in a collection of ten, by over 6,500 people when posted. Our social media channels are regularly seen by over 8,000 people on Facebook and Twitter. This all promotes our already successful website.

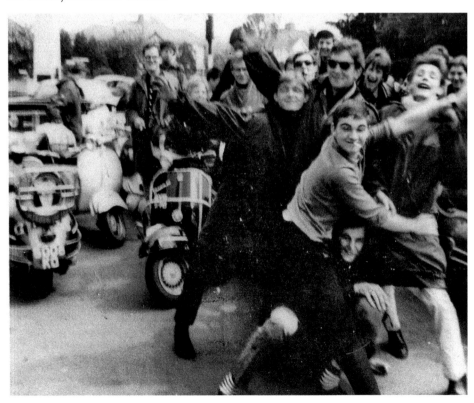

Acknowledgements

This book has been produced with the help of a number of people. We have tried as hard as possible to make it accurate and, in some cases, have corrected mistakes of previous publications. The Orpington History Organisation collection is made up of many other collections and, in the majority of cases, where we have produced an image, we have either the original copy or have permission from the owner. However, it is not always possible to correctly establish the original owner and we apologise in advance for this.

I want to acknowledge and thank the following people for helping with other elements of producing this book:

Keith Baldwin, William Barter, Jean Bodfish, Loraine Budge, Richard Burton, Chris Cartwright, Colin Churcher, Geoffrey Copus, Gretchen Danckwardt, David Daws, Frank Evans, Cllr Peter Fortune, Charles George, Peter Heineke, Christine and Patrick Helicar, Jim Howit, Right Honourable Jo Johnson MP, Marie-Louise Kerr, Philip Lane, LBB Local Studies Department Archive, Simon McKeown, Cllr Peter Morgan, Trevor Mulligan, Suzane North, Sally Pennington, Carol Pitman, Peter Reeve, Lynn Sculpher, George Smith, Jonathan Thompson, Tania Todd, Pam Temple, Sue Turner, Pam Waller, Phil Wheeler.

A special thank you to Tom Yeeles whose help was fundamental in the quality and timely delivery of this book to the publisher.

Posthumous thanks and respect to the late Bill Morton, whose approach to local history was inspiring, and the legacy he has left in his archive has been invaluable to the author, who had the privilege of meeting him on a number of occasions. Bill Morton's archive is available to everyone in the borough and is held at the LBB Local Studies Deptartment.

Bibliography

Copus, Geoffrey, *The Chelsfield Chronicles*
Cox, Dorothy, *The Book of Orpington 1983*
Bromley Public Libraries, *Introduction to the History of Orpington (1975)*
Edwards, John, Morton, Bill, Sign, Tom and Dick Turner, *A Look Back at Orpington*
Farnborough Board Schools, *1873 to 1973, a Short History*
Ford, Marjorie and Geoffrey Rickard, *The Story of Green Street Green*
Hardig, Kathleen and Denise Baldwin, *Along the River Cray; A Pictorial History of the Cray Valley*
Mulligan, Trevor, *Rediscovering the Orpington Car*
Searle, Muriel, *Farnborough and Downe in old picture postcards*
Searle, Muriel and John and Kathleen Warner, *Orpington in old picture postcards*
Shears, W. S., *William Nash of St Paul's Cray, Paper Makers (1967)*
Vinson Close Residents Association, *History on Our Doorstep: A Brief Look at Little Orpington'*
Bromley Borough Local History Society, various issues of *Bromleag* magazine
Waymark, Peter, *A History of Petts Wood*